Conflict
FREE
Living

Conflict FREE Living

JOYCE MEYER

**CHARISMA
HOUSE**

Most CHARISMA HOUSE BOOK GROUP products are available at special quantity discounts for bulk purchase for sales promotions, premiums, fund-raising, and educational needs. For details, write Charisma House Book Group, 600 Rinehart Road, Lake Mary, Florida 32746, or telephone (407) 333-0600.

CONFLICT-FREE LIVING by Joyce Meyer
Published by Charisma House
Charisma Media/Charisma House Book Group
600 Rinehart Road
Lake Mary, Florida 32746
www.charismahouse.com

Unless otherwise noted, all Scripture quotations are from the Amplified Bible. Old Testament copyright © 1965, 1987 by the Zondervan Corporation. The Amplified New Testament copyright © 1954, 1958, 1987 by the Lockman Foundation. Used by permission.

Scripture quotations marked NKJV are from the New King James Version of the Bible. Copyright © 1979, 1980, 1982 by Thomas Nelson, Inc., publishers. Used by permission.

Scripture quotations marked WNT are from the Worrell New Testament. Copyright © 1985 by Gospel Publishing House. Used by permission.

Cover design by Marvin Eans
Design Director: Bill Johnson
Author photograph by Dario Acosta

Visit the author's website at www.joycemeyer.org.

International Standard Book Number: 978-1-61638-651-1
E-book ISBN: 978-1-59979-356-6

The Library of Congress has catalogued the previous edition as follows:

Meyer, Joyce, 1943-
  Conflict-free living / Joyce Meyer.
     p. cm.
  Rev. ed.: Life without strife. 2000.
  Includes bibliographical references.
  ISBN 978-1-59979-062-6
  1. Conflict management--Religious aspects--Christianity. 2.
Interpersonal conflict--Religious aspects--Christianity. 3. Christian
life. I. Meyer, Joyce, 1943- Life without strife. II. Title.
  BV4597.53.C58M48 2008
  248.4--dc22
                              2007032372

12 13 14 15 16 — 9 8 7 6 5 4 3
Printed in the United States of America

Contents

∞

My people are destroyed for lack of knowledge.
—Hosea 4:6

Who is blind but My servant?
—Isaiah 42:19

Introduction

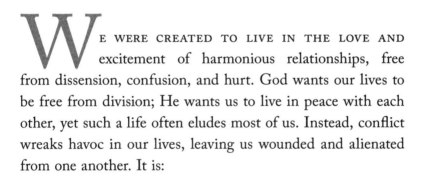

W E WERE CREATED TO LIVE IN THE LOVE AND excitement of harmonious relationships, free from dissension, confusion, and hurt. God wants our lives to be free from division; He wants us to live in peace with each other, yet such a life often eludes most of us. Instead, conflict wreaks havoc in our lives, leaving us wounded and alienated from one another. It is:

- Ending our marriages
- Embittering our children
- Alienating our friends and co-workers
- Splitting our churches
- Bankrupting our health
- Stealing our peace of mind and heart

I know because my life and ministry were once in danger of being destroyed by conflict and strife. My prayer is that as you read the following pages, your eyes will be opened and that you will see, more clearly than ever before, the destructive effects that conflict and dissension can have on your life—and that you will never again fail to recognize strife or confront it.

Jesus gave us His peace for our protection. We are to "hold our peace" and "let peace be the umpire" in every situation (Exod. 14:14; Col. 3:15). We should "crave peace and pursue it" and be "makers and maintainers of peace" (Ps. 34:14; Matt. 5:9).

If we want to experience God's blessing and power, we must resist the devil's attempts to stir up strife.

God's Word contains some wonderful promises for the peaceful, including Psalm 37:37: "Mark the blameless man and behold the upright, for there is a happy end for the man of peace." Think of it. If you are a person of peace—if you learn to resist conflict and strife—you will experience happiness. God says that His children will inherit righteousness, peace, and joy. The kingdom of God consists of these three things, but few who claim Christ as their Savior actually experience these benefits in their everyday lives. Satan deceives, lies, and beguiles believers through a lack of knowledge or the unwillingness to apply the knowledge we have.

God has instructed us to put on the full armor of God so that we can defeat the devil in every one of his strategies and deceits. (See Ephesians 6:10–18.) If we want to experience God's blessing and power, we must resist the devil's attempts to stir up strife. We must be on guard, because "the devil roams around like a lion roaring [in fierce hunger], seeking someone to seize upon and devour" (1 Pet. 5:8).

If relationship problems have plagued your life, then this book is for you. If you are wondering why you don't experience spiritual power in your life and ministry, even though you are serving God and doing all you know to do, then this book is for you. If you are confused about why you are missing out on the blessings that God promises to His children, then this book is for you.

In it we are going to explore why so many of our relationships are the opposite of what Jesus promised and what we can do to enjoy the life God wants us to have. In part 1 you will learn how to recognize strife so that you can, in turn, resist it. In part 2 you will discover how to heal your troubled relationships. And in part 3, you will learn how you can unleash God's power and blessing in your life.

At the end of each chapter you will find a section devoted to summary and reflection. This section is designed to help you apply the insights you learn in each chapter. It will give you dynamic keys for discerning the roots and symptoms of conflict and strife so that you can enjoy trouble-free relationships.

Read on, and learn how your life and relationships can be full of harmony and power and blessing.

Part I

Identifying the Telltale Signs

one

Why Is My Life
So Difficult?

∞

ONE EVENING MY HUSBAND, DAVE, AND I WERE going to pick up another couple to take them out to dinner. We had only been to their home one time, and it had been quite awhile since that first visit. On our way there, Dave turned to me and said, "I don't think I remember how to get to the house."

"Oh, well, I do!" I promptly told him, and then proceeded to give him directions.

"I really don't think that is the right way to go," he said.

"Dave, you never listen to me!" I said. My tone and body language let him know that I did not appreciate his challenging me. At my persistence, Dave finally agreed to follow my directions. I told him that our friends lived in a brown

1

house on a cul-de-sac at the end of such-and-such street. As we drove, I gave him directions for all the turns.

As our car turned onto the street where I believed the house to be, I noticed a bicycle lying on the sidewalk. "I know this is the right street," I said, "because I remember that bicycle lying there the last time we were here!" We drove to the end of the street and—guess what! No brown house. No cul-de-sac. I was as wrong as wrong could be.

I wish I could say that this was an isolated incident. I can't. I created havoc in my life and in my relationships for many years and was a very difficult person to get along with. I was always in conflict with something or someone. I loved God, was born again, was baptized in the Holy Spirit, and had a call on my life to full-time ministry, but I was also very wounded and very angry.

I grew up in a violent and angry home, and my entire child-hood was filled with fear, embarrassment, and shame. My father sexually, physically, verbally, and emotionally abused me from the time I was three until I left home at eighteen. He never physically forced me to submit to him, but he did force me to pretend I liked what he was doing. He used anger and intimidation to control other family members and me.

When I turned eighteen, I moved out of my parents' home while my father was away at work one day. Shortly after that, I married the first young man who showed any interest in me. My first husband was a manipulator, a thief, and a con man who was usually unemployed. He once abandoned me in California with nothing but a dime and a carton of soda bottles.

The abuse, violence, lies, and manipulation I endured left me feeling out of control, but of course I could not admit that. Nor could I admit the intense rage I felt. I was bitter toward life and people. I resented those who had nice lives and had not endured the pain I had. I did not know how to receive God's love, grace, and mercy—or anyone else's.

Even after I married Dave, I continued to do everything I could to control the people and circumstances of my life so that I would never be hurt so deeply again. Of course, that didn't work very well. All of my relationships were strained and stressful, and I couldn't understand why.

Like me, many people are experiencing the devastation of strife, but they don't recognize it as the root cause of their problems.

Nor could I understand why my ministry wasn't growing and being blessed, despite all Dave's and my efforts and prayers. But as I began to grow in my relationship with the Lord, He began to work in my life. As I studied the Word and all the promises it gives us about peace, I came to want that for my life, and the Holy Spirit began to show me that strife was the cause of my problems. I learned to recognize it and to resist it. I now treat strife as a dangerous foe that will bring destruction if left unconfronted.

Like me, many people are experiencing the devastation of strife, but they don't recognize it as the root cause of their problems. They blame others or Satan and don't realize that they have the power to say yes or no to conflict and strife. Instead of keeping strife out, they are holding open the door to conflict, all the time wondering why their lives are so difficult.

Learning to Recognize Strife

The dictionary defines *strife* as "fighting; heated, often violent conflict; bitter dissension; a struggle between rivals; or contention."* Other descriptive words that describe strife are *quarrel, rivalry, wrangling, debate, provocation,* and *factions.* I define *strife* as a bickering, arguing, heated disagreement, or an angry undercurrent.

The Bible has much to say about strife and contention (which are actually the same thing) and points to strife as the source of many other kinds of problems. The apostle James wrote, "For wherever there is jealousy (envy) and contention (rivalry and selfish ambition), there will also be confusion (unrest, disharmony, rebellion) and all sorts of evil and vile practices" (James 3:16). And we read in Hebrews 12:14–15, "Strive to live in peace with everybody and pursue that consecration and holiness without which no one will [ever] see the Lord. Exercise foresight and be on the watch to look [after one another], to see that no one falls back from and fails to secure God's grace (His unmerited favor and spiritual blessing), *in order that no root of resentment (rancor, bitterness, or hatred) shoots forth and causes trouble and bitter torment, and the many become contaminated and defiled by it*" (emphasis added).

Strife leads to resentment, rancor, bitterness, or hatred. Left unconfronted, it destroys and devastates. It causes trouble and brings torment to church members and to church leadership, hindering God's work and contaminating many.

If a deadly plague should strike a household, the Department

---

* *New Riverside University Dictionary* (Boston, MA: The Riverside Publishing Company, 1994), s.v. "strife."

of Health would place the household in quarantine. Public notices would announce that the house is contaminated. No one would be allowed in or near the house for fear they would be contaminated and defiled also. We need to be as vigilant when it comes to eliminating strife.

That's why it's so important to learn how to identify the symptoms of strife, including:

- Pride (or defensiveness)
- Bitterness
- Hatred
- Judgment and criticism
- Deception and lies
- Anger
- Rebellion
- Unrest
- Fear and negativity

Anytime we give in to any of these feelings, we open the door to strife and usher in destruction. Strife kills! It kills the anointing, the blessings, the prosperity, the peace, and the joy.

Strife is not just a problem between people; it's often a problem within a person. What is going on inside of you? Is the atmosphere inside peaceful or tense? Strife can, and often does, affect our attitude first. One day I overheard a woman railing on and on about the postal system and the post office. After listening to her about late mail deliveries, lost packages, and the cost of postage, I thought, "This woman's anger has robbed her of peace and joy." As long as she was so angry at the post office, she certainly could never enjoy going to the post office. Even talking about it upset her.

Strife often gains entrance through a minor issue, something that really doesn't make a difference. For example, a friend makes a passing comment about how she liked our old hairstyle better, and we take offense. But instead of talking about it with the friend and making peace, or extending grace, we choose to replay the words over and over in our minds, feeding our anger, and thereby ushering strife into our life. We continue giving in to strife, and before we know it, we seem constantly enraged.

While strife typically gains entrance into our lives through a person, that isn't always the case. Sometimes our conflict can be with a place. Several years ago I purchased a dress at a store, and the dress fell apart not long afterward. When I tried to return it, the salesperson refused to take it back. I was very upset because I felt it was unfair, and I told everybody I talked to about this store and their poor customer service. I enthusiastically discouraged anyone who would listen from going there to shop. Every time I passed the store while walking in the shopping mall, I would begin to feel upset. If anyone was with me, I would repeat the story and get even more upset.

God began to show me that I needed to forgive that salesperson and even the dress shop for its policies that did not leave room to meet my need. This was a new level of learning for me regarding forgiveness. I knew about forgiving people, but not places. I learned that being in strife with a place is just as dangerous as being in strife with a person. The only difference is that a place has no feelings, but the effect on the person in strife is just as destructive.

If we fail to recognize and resist strife, it poisons our attitudes and begins to negatively affect all of our relationships—our relationships at school, work, home, and church. What's worse is that we often have no idea when the problems even started or what to do about them.

This was the case for a woman who approached me after one of my meetings. She told me that after hearing me preach on strife, she had purchased the entire teaching album on strife and began a study of the subject. She said that her family had a long history of conflict and divorces, with brother mad at brother, sister mad at sister, and children hating parents. The night she heard me speak, God revealed to her the cause of the troubled relationships that seemed to plague her and her relatives: they had failed to resist strife. Consequently, family gatherings were filled with dissension and an undercurrent of anger.

Strife often gains entrance through a minor issue, something that really doesn't make a difference.

She said that she didn't want to live in a state of conflict anymore, so she had listened to the tape series and learned to recognize strife and to resist it. Over time, her life and relationships became more peaceful. Not only that, but she also shared what she had learned with many of her relatives, and they had learned to shut the door on strife and conflict as well. One by one many of them were set free because they had learned the truth about the destructive nature of strife. Jesus said, "If you abide in My word, you are My disciples indeed. And you shall know the truth, and the truth shall make you free" (John 8:31–32, NKJV).

Confronting Strife, Embracing Peace

Strife spreads like an infection or a highly contagious disease. Many become contaminated and defiled by it. That's why Dave and I work hard to keep it out of our home. Because our personalities are very different, we often do not think alike on issues or see things in the same way. Still, we have learned to talk calmly through our disagreements, being careful not to let pride, resentment, bitterness, jealousy, or anger come between us. When we see symptoms of strife in our relationship, we immediately confront them and restore peace between us.

We also make a concerted effort to keep divisiveness out of Joyce Meyer Ministries. When people come to work for us, we tell them during their training that we will not tolerate strife. We teach them to be aware of the symptoms of strife, such as judgment and criticism, so that they will close the door to strife and learn to take their opinions to the Lord or to the person responsible for their complaint—not to other employees. We train them to walk in love with other employees, being abundant in mercy and quick to overlook an offense. We want our home and our ministry to be places where peace and harmony reign.

Do you?

I pray that by the end of this book you will be so hungry for peace that you will do whatever you need to do to keep strife out of your life. If you must strive at something, strive to keep strife out. Be diligent.

I recently received a letter from a couple who had attended a meeting we hosted in Florida. They wrote that for the first twenty-seven years of their married life, conflict and strife characterized their relationship. Although they were Christians who loved each other, they had never been able to have peace in their relationship. They bickered, argued, and could not get along. They knew well the truth of Proverbs 17:1: "Better is a dry morsel with quietness, than a house full of feasting with strife" (NKJV). Ironically, they were involved in a counseling ministry to married couples at their church, yet they themselves lived under condemnation because they could not do in their lives what they were teaching others.

They wrote: "We reached a breakthrough because of your teaching on strife. We never really knew what the problem was. But now we do, and because of that revelation, we can live in victory."

Strife does not have to destroy your life. If you desire to walk in victory, do what this couple did. It's not too late. Learn to recognize the spirit of strife and confront it. Refuse to be fuel for it, so that you can claim the righteousness, peace, and joy that are rightfully yours as a child of God.

Chapter 1
Summary and Reflection

In order to experience peaceful and harmonious relationships, we need to remember that victory over conflict and strife requires us to engage in a spiritual battle. Ephesians 6:12 says, "We are not wrestling with flesh and blood [contending only with physical opponents], but against the despotisms, against the powers, against [the master spirits who are] the world rulers of this present darkness, against the spirit forces of wickedness in the heavenly (supernatural) sphere."

1. Define *strife* in your own words.

_____

_____

_____

_____

2. We've all been in circumstances that are full of tension and conflict. Describe some symptoms of a strife-filled...

Home

_____

_____

Church

_____

_____

_____

Workplace

_____

_____

Other situation

_____

_____

3. Think about the relationships that you struggle with, whether at home (with your parents and siblings, spouse and kids), at school or work, or at church. Ask God to show you where the following characteristics of strife have opened the door for a specific conflict in those relationships. What did you say or think that was motivated by…

Pride (Were you often defensive? Did you insist on having the last word? Were you more interested in making your point than in learning God's perspective on the matter?)

_____

_____

_____

Bitterness (Did you use phrases such as "you always" or "you never," which are symptoms of hidden bitterness?)

_____

_____

_____

Hatred

_____

_____

Judgment and criticism (Did you assign motives and intentions to another person when it is not possible to really know another's heart? Did you make judgments in other ways?)

_____

_____

Deception and lies (Did you misunderstand the situation from the other person's point of view, or did you form an opinion without knowing all the facts? Did you form opinions based on gossip? Did you lie or bend the truth in any way?)

_____

_____

Anger

_____

_____

Unrest (Did you say or do something out of worry or anxiety?)

_____

_____

Fear and negativity (Did you say or do something out of fear or negativity?)

_____

_____

4. Are you in strife with yourself? Describe how any of the above characteristics apply to your thoughts or how you see yourself.

_____

_____

5. In what ways have conflict and strife brought devastation and destruction into your life?

_____

_____

6. How might your life change if you sought to heal any troubled relationships and resist strife?

_____

_____

_____

_____

_____

Lord, help me to recognize strife and learn to resist it. Help me to see the entrance of the spirit of strife long before it wreaks havoc in my home and life. Supply the grace to me so that I never fuel the spirit of strife in my life or in the lives of others. Amen.

two

I'm Right and *You're* Wrong

∞

HAVE YOU EVER BEEN ABSOLUTELY SURE YOU WERE correct about something? Your mind appeared to have a store of facts and details to prove you were right—but you ended up being wrong. What did you do? Did you admit your error, or did you keep pushing and trying to find a way to defend your position?

In the past, when my husband and I were watching a movie or television show, we often argued over which actors and actresses were portraying the characters. It seemed to me that Dave thought Henry Fonda played half the characters in movies.

"Oh, look," he'd say as we watched a movie on television. "Henry Fonda is in this movie."

"That's not Henry Fonda," I'd answer back, and we'd start arguing and bickering. Both of us were so intent on being right that we would insist on staying up much later than we should, just so we could see the credits roll at the end. Then one of us could say, "I told you so!"

Why do we want so desperately to be right about things? Why is it so difficult to be wrong? Why is it so important for us to "win" in a disagreement?

Pride wants desperately to look good, to look intelligent, to be admired—even to ourselves.

For years I felt bad about who I was, and in order to feel any confidence at all, I had to be right all the time. So I would argue and go to great extremes to prove it. Someone was always challenging me, and I lived in frustration as I tried to convince everyone that I knew what I was talking about.

It wasn't until my identity became rooted and grounded in Christ that I began to experience freedom in this area. Now I know that my worth and value do not come from appearing right to others. They are found in the fact that Jesus loved me enough to die for me and bring me into a personal relationship with Him.

Why did I have to be right? Because my pride was at stake. Pride wants desperately to look good, to look intelligent, to be admired—even to ourselves. So much so that, as Obadiah 3 tells us, "The pride of your heart has deceived you." Pride can deceive us and make us think we are right when we are actually wrong.

Pride wants desperately to please the flesh—at any cost. The flesh, if not under the control of the Holy Spirit, does all in its power to have its own way: "Give me what I want, when I want it, the way I want it, and do it now!" This is the cry of all of us, apart from the Spirit of God.

Pride cannot lead us into victory. There is no hope of peace without a willingness to humble ourselves. The Word of God teaches that pride leads us into destruction. "Pride goes before destruction, and a haughty spirit before a fall" (Prov. 16:18). Pride seeks to tear the other down in order to build itself up. When we have pride in our hearts, our words often become judgmental and divisive, causing all sorts of dissatisfaction and problems in our relationships.

Arrogant Hearts, Divisive Words

Words are containers for power. But they can carry either creative or destructive power. They carry the power of God or the power of Satan. "A soft answer turns away wrath, but grievous words stir up anger" (Prov. 15:1), and "A gentle tongue [with its healing power] is a tree of life" (v. 4). A soft answer brings peace into the midst of turmoil. A gentle tongue has healing power.

James warns us about the power of the tongue to cause hurt and division: "And the tongue is a fire. [The tongue is a] world of wickedness set among our members, contaminating and depraving the whole body and setting on fire the wheel of birth (the cycle of man's nature), being itself ignited by hell (Gehenna)" (James 3:6).

Wrong words or words spoken at the wrong time can certainly start a fire, particularly when they are words of judgment, criticism, gossip, and talebearing. Judgment says, "You are defective, but I am not."

An example of the destruction caused by arrogance and judgment can be found in Luke 18:10–14:

"Two men went up into the temple [enclosure] to pray, the one a Pharisee and the other a tax collector. The Pharisee took his stand ostentatiously and began to pray thus before and with himself: God, I thank You that I am not like the rest of men— extortioners (robbers), swindlers [unrighteous in heart and life], adulterers—or even like this tax collector here. I fast twice a week; I give tithes of all that I gain.

"But the tax collector, [merely] standing at a distance, would not even lift up his eyes to heaven, but kept striking his breast, saying, O God, be favorable (be gracious, be merciful) to me, the especially wicked sinner that I am!

Notice that pride will even follow us into the prayer closet.

"I tell you, this man went down to his home justified (forgiven and made upright and in right standing with God), rather than the other man; for everyone who exalts himself will be humbled, but he who humbles himself will be exalted."

Notice that pride will even follow us into the prayer closet. We tell ourselves that we are praying about someone else's faults, but we may actually be operating out of a critical and judgmental spirit, which Jesus condemns.

But before our pride causes us to point a judgmental finger at the Pharisee in this parable, let me ask you a question. Aren't we sometimes guilty of the same when it comes to discussing the Bible? One person thinks one thing, and another believes something else. We tell each other, "Your interpretation is wrong." We each keep pushing our points and trying to convince the other. Soon words are said that can't be taken back, and relationships are damaged.

A while ago we hired three new employees at Joyce Meyer Ministries, all very young and in need of some years to grow up in the Lord. Soon after they began, I received reports that other employees in their department sensed conflict and division among the three new employees as a result of their debates on various portions of the Bible. Dave and I talked with the three employees, and, happily, they received our correction. The door of debate was closed, and the strife ceased.

Judgmental arguments that arise about Scripture are the result of spiritual pride. This is the most disgusting kind of pride to the Lord.

So be on your guard, as Satan loves it when Christians are divisive. Paul wrote to the Christians at Ephesus, "We are not wrestling with flesh and blood [contending only with physical opponents], but against the despotisms, against the powers, against [the master spirits who are] the world rulers of this present darkness, against the spirit forces of wickedness in the heavenly (supernatural) sphere" (Eph. 6:12).

If we want to defeat Satan and enjoy trouble-free relationships, we will exchange pride for humility, keep our mouths shut, and follow the prompting of the Holy Spirit.

Exchange Pride for Humility

If we are not willing to humble ourselves, we have no hope of peaceful relationships. As long as we think we know everything, we do not know anything. When we believe we still have a lot to learn and stop passing out our opinions, we have finally come to the place where knowledge can begin. The apostle Paul stated, "For I resolved to know nothing (to be acquainted with nothing, to make a display of the knowledge of nothing, and to be conscious of nothing) among you except Jesus Christ (the Messiah) and Him crucified" (1 Cor. 2:2).

Not only was Paul a Pharisee, but he also called himself the "son of Pharisees" (Acts 23:6). He was one of the chief Pharisees and was extremely well educated. Yet he says he would rather forget all he ever thought he knew in order to "know...Jesus Christ (the Messiah) and Him crucified." Over the years, I have found that I have to be nailed to the cross with Jesus regularly if I am going to stay out of pride. I too have to know Christ and Him crucified.

If we want to defeat Satan and enjoy trouble-free relationships, we will exchange pride for humility, keep our mouths shut, and follow the prompting of the Holy Spirit.

Too often we don't understand statements like this in the Word of God, so we pass over them and miss a very important lesson. The Book of Romans says we will not reign with Christ if we do not suffer with Him: "And if we are [His] children, then we are [His] heirs also: heirs of God and fellow heirs with Christ [sharing His inheritance with

Him]; only we must share His suffering if we are to share His glory" (Rom. 8:17). (We'll talk more about what this means in chapter 15.)

I now enjoy the glory of a peaceful life, but I had to go through the suffering of learning to crucify my pride. I also had to learn to stop arguing.

Keep Our Mouth Shut

Wrong words are like fuel on a fire. The more fuel we pour on the fire, the bigger the fire grows. The only way to stop the inflammation is to remove the fuel. The only way to stop or prevent a disagreement or argument is to stop speaking. When someone insults us or hurts our feelings, we are often tempted to give a response out of our wounded pride. But it would be wiser to ignore the insult and let God deal with the person. We must give up wanting to prove that we are right and everyone else is wrong.

It's ironic that many of our arguments are over insignificant concerns. The apostle Paul warns us about such conversations in 2 Timothy 2:23–24: "But refuse (shut your mind against, have nothing to do with) trifling (ill-informed, unedifying, stupid) controversies over ignorant questionings, for you know that they foster strife and breed quarrels. And the servant of the Lord must not be quarrelsome (fighting and contending). Instead, he must be kindly to everyone and mild-tempered [preserving the bond of peace]; he must be a skilled and suitable teacher, patient and forbearing and willing to suffer wrong."

Notice the word *trifling* in verse 23. It indicates things that are unimportant and make no difference when considered with things that are really important. I believe the verse is really saying, "Stay out of conversations where no one knows what they are talking about and everybody is arguing over nothing." So often our pride keeps us arguing over things that make no difference to anybody. A proud heart refuses to be quiet because pride demands that I have my say—I must have the last word.

I have always been an expert at trying to convince others that my way was the right way, but as the Holy Spirit has convicted me in this area, I have learned to shut my mouth when I find myself in the middle of a disagreement. I know that I must back down, be quiet, and trust God to take care of the situation. Believe me, I have avoided a lot of arguments by refusing to stoke the fire of strife with my words. My relationships and life are much more peaceful when I allow the Holy Spirit to do the convincing!

When someone insults us or hurts our feelings, pride tempts us to give a response out of our wounded emotions. But I would rather live in peace than get my own way all the time. Wouldn't you?

Follow the Prompting of the Holy Spirit

Both Dave and I have learned to listen to the Holy Spirit in this area. There are times when we just do not agree. My husband is not a difficult person to get along with. As a matter of fact, he is very adaptable and accommodating. But there are certain issues that both of us feel very strongly about, and no one is going to convince either of us that we are wrong, except for God Himself.

Sometimes God convinces Dave, and sometimes He convinces me. If I press the issue, trying to convince Dave, the harmony in our relationship is destroyed, and strife enters our lives. If I humble myself under the mighty hand of God and wait on Him,

I have learned that He, and He alone, is able to convince my husband in certain situations.

Now whenever Dave and I are tempted to defend our pride by insisting that we are right, God has enabled us to say, "I think I am right, but I may be wrong." It is absolutely amazing how many arguments we have avoided over the years by using that simple act of humility. I have found that when I obey the Holy Spirit's prompting, a relationship can become harmonious once again.

I have learned that even when wrong words ignite a flame, right words can put it out.

Of course, there are times when we should speak up and confront people, but it's vital that we are sensitive to the Spirit of God in each situation. Sometimes I am all fired up and want to tell someone that he or she will not mistreat me or take advantage of me any longer. But no matter how much I want to confront that individual, the Holy Spirit persistently tells me to leave it alone.

Other times I do not want to speak with a person about an issue, but God lets me know that I must. When this is the case, I choose my words carefully so that I speak out of wisdom rather than emotion. I am cautiously aware of the impact of voice tones and body language. I have learned that even when wrong words ignite a flame, right words can put it out.

The Book of Proverbs tells us, "There are those who speak rashly, like the piercing of a sword, but the tongue of the wise brings healing" (Prov. 12:18). Also, "A fool's wrath is quickly and openly known, but a prudent man ignores an insult" (Prov. 12:16).

Our Model

If we want to enjoy trouble-free, harmonious relationships, we will follow Jesus's example. He was accused of wrongdoing regularly, yet never once did He attempt to defend Himself. He let people think He was wrong, and it did not disturb Him at all.

He could do so because He knew who He was. He did not have a problem with His self-image. He was not trying to prove anything. He trusted His heavenly Father to vindicate Him, and we can do the same.

Give your need to be right over to God, and watch your relationships improve. You'll discover that great spiritual power is released in unity and harmony.

Chapter 2
Summary and Reflection

Many of our relationship problems are due to pride. Pride gets us to fight to be right. It will fill our minds with self-deception. We will be able to justify all kinds of wrong attitudes and behaviors, all the while being fully convinced that we are right.

The Bible says in James 3:14, "But if you have bitter jealousy (envy) and contention (rivalry, selfish ambition) in your hearts, do not pride yourselves on it and thus be in defiance of and false to the Truth."

1. Search your own heart and think very honestly about a time when you became embroiled in strife. Did you justify your actions? Describe that time.

   _____

   _____

   _____

2. Pride and deception go together. Asking the Holy Spirit to help you, recall a time in your life when your pride convinced you that you were right, but you were deceived nevertheless. Describe that time.

   _____

   _____

   _____

3. The Bible says that the tongue is a fire (James 3:6). Describe a situation in which your pride caused you to say something

that stirred up strife with another person. How did your words inflame the situation?

_____

_____

_____

4. Now, imagine how that situation may have turned out differently if you had exchanged your pride for humility. What could you have said instead that would have quenched the fire of strife?

_____

_____

_____

5. Describe a time when the Holy Spirit was prompting you to say or do something that would have prevented or ended a conflict with someone. Did you obey His prompting or not? What happened as a result?

_____

_____

_____

6. A certain amount of suffering is necessary to grace us to swallow our pride. Describe a situation in which you swallowed your pride and resisted strife.

_____

_____

_____

_____

Lord, I surrender to You my need to defend self, explain self, empower self, and to always be right. I acknowledge that You alone are the only One who is right. And even if I feel right about some situations, it never justifies strife. I submit my life to You completely, and I choose to let You alone be my defender.

three

God, I Don't See Your Power and Blessing in My Life

∞

D O YOU WONDER WHY YOU ARE NOT PROSPERING, even though you are giving to God and serving Him? Are you pouring your life and time into your church or ministry, yet failing to see it grow in numbers and spiritual power? If you answered yes to either of these questions, it may be because of the presence of conflict and strife in your life, whether it be in your home, workplace, or ministry.

In the beginning years of our ministry, Dave and I did a lot of religious or spiritual things, but we lacked peace in our home. Everything would be fine one minute, and the next thing I knew, everyone would be mad—screaming and yelling. Or we would experience the other extreme, everyone would be deathly quiet—so cold and quiet that it was obvious feelings were hurt and wrong thoughts were running rampant.

I can remember our family arguing all the way to church on Sunday mornings, but living in pretense that all was well as soon as we saw anyone we knew. I would "fake" my way through the service, putting on my "church face" and clapping at all the right places, saying "Amen!" at the appropriate times, and pretending to pay attention to the pastor while he preached. All the while, I was planning how I would ignore Dave or the kids until they apologized to me. I certainly did not intend to go home and fix them a nice dinner. I really didn't even plan to talk to them.

Dave and I often talked about power, prosperity, healing, and success in those days, but we did not possess those things. It was as if we were window-shopping. We could see what God said was rightfully ours, but we didn't know how to get those blessings into our hands.

We even tried praying the prayer of agreement, because it says in Matthew 18:19, "Again I tell you, if two of you on earth agree (harmonize together, make a symphony together) about whatever [anything and everything] they may ask, it will come to pass and be done for them by My Father in heaven."

However, even after praying this prayer, we failed to see the powerful results we had been taught that we could have. Then God revealed to us that He is not pleased or satisfied with religious sacrifices in a house full of strife. "Better is a dry morsel with quietness than a house full of feasting [on offered sacrifices] with strife" (Prov. 17:1). He is not looking for phony Christians. He wants the real thing—not just people who "talk the talk," but those who "walk the walk."

God responds to the prayer of agreement when it is prayed by people who agree. If Dave and I had been fighting all week, there was no power in joining hands, bowing our heads, and coming together in order to move God. The prayer of agreement is only effective when prayed by those who "harmonize together, make a symphony together."

God told us, "Keep the strife out of your life, out of your home, and out of your ministry. Walk in integrity, and do what you do with excellence."

Once God exposed the strife in our lives, I began to see a pattern. Not only did our family tend to get into arguments on Sunday morning while we were on our way to church, I also noticed that Dave and I would often have some kind of conflict just before a seminar where we would be ministering. It became obvious to me that Satan was stirring up dissension in order to keep us from hearing God's Word and moving forward spiritually. He was using strife to block the anointing in my life and ministry.

Strife Blocks God's Power

The Bible teaches us that the seed of God's Word must be sown in a heart of peace by someone who works for and makes peace. James wrote, "And the harvest of righteousness (of conformity to God's will in thought and deed) is [the fruit of the seed] sown in peace by those who work for and make peace [in themselves and in others, that peace which means concord, agreement, and harmony between individuals, with undisturbedness, in a peaceful mind free from fears and agitating passions and moral conflicts]" (James 3:18).

As a minister, this means that I must stay in peace myself and be a peacemaker if I desire a strong anointing flowing forth from me to help people.

As we travel and minister in various churches, I have found it interesting to note how often pastors come to church in separate cars from the rest of their families. At first, I thought this was a bit unusual, but some of them shared a twofold reason for doing so. First, many pastors like to get to the church early to pray and meditate on their sermon. And second, they want to be peaceful when they get there, and they have found that it is easier to stay peaceful if they drive by themselves.

The Bible also teaches that the enemy comes immediately after the seed is sown, hoping to steal the Word: "The sower sows the Word. The ones along the path are those who have the Word sown [in their hearts], but when they hear, Satan comes at once and [by force] takes away the message which is sown in them" (Mark 4:14–15).

God responds to the prayer of agreement when it is prayed by people who agree.

Satan is intent on stealing the Word before it takes root in us. He knows that if it takes root in our hearts, it will begin to produce good fruit. We must operate in the wisdom of God from within and show ourselves wiser than the enemy. We cannot sit by passively and allow the devil to get us so upset before we get to church that we cannot hear or retain what is being said.

Nor can we allow him to get us upset after we leave. In order to grow spiritually, we need to be able to think about the Word that has been preached and taught to us. Jesus said, "Be careful what you are hearing. The measure [of thought and study] you give [to the truth you hear] will be the measure [of virtue and knowledge] that comes back to you—and more [besides] will be given to you who hear" (Mark 4:24).

No matter how anointed a speaker is, that anointing will have no effect on you if you're in strife when you hear God's Word.

Strife not only blocks spirit power, but it also blocks God's blessings.

Strife Blocks God's Blessing

Many believers are seeking prosperity. They go to seminars on prosperity and read books on prosperity and success. This is good, for we need to be instructed and informed, but the Bible clarifies why prosperity eludes some people. It certainly eluded our family for a long while. We had all the right head knowledge—we gave and confessed and believed—but we were also living in strife and didn't have any idea that it was blocking our blessing. Strife kills God's blessing and power. I've seen this over and over again.

I once heard the story of a Christian couple who lost everything they had in a fire. Everyone who knew them was confused by the loss, because outwardly, this couple seemed to be living the perfect Christian life. They were doing everything right.

Both of them had just graduated from a Bible college, and they were preparing to go into full-time ministry. They had a bumper sticker, a tape recorder, and sermon tapes; they wore a Jesus pin. They knew the Word and said all the right things. So, the tragedy left questions in the minds of their friends and acquaintances. How could this happen to people who were walking in faith?

You may know of similar cases. Keep in mind that we do not know what goes on behind closed doors. It remains unseen. This couple later admitted that God had been dealing with them about their marriage relationship and the dissension and conflict in their home, but they had not humbled themselves and come into obedience.

Again, a house full of sacrifices, yet with strife, does not please the Lord. This young couple may have been sacrificing to go to Bible college, but none of the offerings of their flesh were satisfactory compensation for the door they had opened to the devil through their disobedience and strife. This couple knew the right thing to do. They knew that God was telling them to resist strife and live in harmony with each other. The Lord had been dealing with them, but they had not been heeding His warnings. Therefore, the devil took advantage of the open door and brought destruction.

I knew another couple who tithed and attended church regularly, yet they had continual problems with sickness, poverty, broken appliances, and car repairs. They had no victory. After years of struggle and problems, they finally revealed in a counseling session that they had so much animosity and strife between them that they had not slept together as man and wife for years.

Conflict and strife block God's blessings. But where there is unity, there will God command His blessings.

The Bottom Line

We have many promises in God's Word that He will bless and prosper us. For example: "Behold, how good and how pleasant it is for brethren to dwell together in unity! It is like the precious ointment poured on the head, that ran down on the beard, even the beard of Aaron [the first high priest], that came down upon the collar and skirts of his garments [consecrating the whole body]. It is like the dew of [lofty] Mount Hermon and the dew that comes on the hills of Zion; for there the Lord has commanded the blessing, even life forevermore [upon the high and the lowly]" (Ps. 133:1–3).

I love this psalm. It verifies what I am trying to teach. Life is enjoyable when people live in unity and keep strife out of their lives. On the other hand, there is nothing worse than a home or relationship filled with an angry undercurrent of strife.

Perhaps that's why unity is one of the last things Jesus talked about with His disciples before He was arrested and crucified. During the Last Supper He prayed, "That they all may be one, [just] as You, Father, are in Me and I in You, that they also may be one in Us, so that the world may believe and be convinced that You have sent Me" (John 17:21).

You might be able to learn a lot about how to give your testimony or preach a sermon by going to Bible college. You might be able to give the message of salvation by memorizing Bible verses or by listening to teaching CDs while driving in your car. You might even be able to spread awareness of our Savior by wearing a Jesus pin on your clothes. However, if you do all this, yet you are living in strife rather than in unity, your life will lack spiritual power and blessing.

Many frequently live in confusion, wondering why the promises of God don't work in their lives. The promises of God cannot just be "claimed." They must be inherited as we enter into a "sonship" relationship with our Father. The "sons of God" are those who are "led by the Spirit of God" (Rom. 8:14–15).

If you are wondering why you aren't experiencing more of God's power and blessing in your life, look at your relationships. Do you have problems with your spouse, your children, your co-workers, or your fellow believers? Are you party to conflict in your church or on the job?

While it can be tempting to get ourselves off the hook by refusing to look at the "why" behind the "what" when our lives lack the things God has promised us, we must be willing to do so if we want the life God offers.

Trials come for a variety of reasons. Disobedience is one of them. You may have problems that have nothing to do with disobedience or strife. The devil may be simply attacking you, trying to destroy your faith. If you steadfastly resist him, you will come into a place of victory. On the other hand, it is possible that troubled relationships may be the root of your trouble.

If you are wondering why you aren't experiencing more of God's power and blessing in your life, look at your relationships.

You may not be able to walk in peace with every single person you know. If so, don't be afraid that God will not be able to bless you. The Word says, "If possible, as far as it depends on you, live at peace with everyone" (Rom. 12:18). As you face the truth, learn to resist strife, and live in harmony with others, God will free you to live the life you were made to live. If you are a peacemaker, God's blessing and power will flow to you.

Chapter 3
Summary and Reflection

Many people are seeking prosperity and want the power of God in their lives. The Word of God tells us what is required if we want these things: "God is faithful (reliable, trustworthy, and therefore ever true to His promise, and He can be depended on); by Him you were called into companionship and participation with His Son, Jesus Christ our Lord. But I urge and entreat you, brethren, by the name of our Lord Jesus Christ, that all of you be in perfect harmony and full agreement in what you say, and that there be no dissensions or factions or divisions among you, but that you be perfectly united in your common understanding and in your opinions and judgments. For it has been made clear to me, my brethren, by those of Chloe's household, that there are contentions *[strife]* and wrangling and factions among you" (1 Cor. 1:9–11).

1. Do you see God's power and blessings in your life? If so, in what ways? If not, look at your relationships. What do you see that might be hindering the flow of God's blessing in your life?

   _____

   _____

   _____

2. Describe what happens in your house on Sunday mornings and when you are returning home from church. Do you see a pattern? Is the enemy trying to steal God's Word before it can

be planted into your heart? Do you often have quarrels and squabbles?

_____

_____

_____

3. What strategies can you employ in the future to break this pattern and establish harmonious relationships?

_____

_____

_____

4. God requires obedience to His powerful Word. In light of our discussion about conflict and strife, rewrite the following verse in your own words. Jesus prayed, "That they all may be one, [just] as You, Father, are in Me and I in You, that they also may be in one in Us, so that the world may believe and be convinced that You have sent Me" (John 17:21).

_____

_____

_____

5. Think back to a time when you personally experienced the kind of unity spoken about in 1 Corinthians 1:9–11. How did you experience God's power or blessing in that situation?

_____

_____

_____

6. We may have problems that have nothing whatsoever to do with strife. On the other hand, we may be burdened with problems that have entered our lives through the door of strife. What

challenging situations or problems in your life have been caused by strife?

_____

_____

_____

Lord, show me how to diffuse potentially strife-filled situations. Help me recognize any patterns of strife in my relationships, particularly those that may be hindering my spiritual growth and blocking your power and blessing in my life. Help me choose the godly wisdom of harmony, unity, and peace. Show me how I can restore peace in relationships broken or damaged through offenses and misunderstandings. I make a new commitment to become a peacemaker whenever possible with Your help. Amen.

four

The Pastor Must Not Like Me

❧

Y EARS AGO WHEN DAVE AND I FIRST BECAME CHRIS- tians, we attended a charismatic church that was only a few months old. The congregation was growing quickly, and the attendance had already reached four hundred or more people. The gifts of the Spirit were evident, and God's anointing and fresh revelation were flowing to the people. Everything seemed to be the way it should be. But today the church is no longer in existence. What happened?

Strife got in! The devil is a supreme strategist, and he works hard to get believers upset with each other because he knows that the Holy Spirit will only work in an atmosphere of peace. If the devil can stir up trouble in a church, he effec- tively shuts down the work of God in that place, which is his goal. So he lays out a plan and does not mind working behind the scenes for long periods of time. He lies to people, pitting them against each other. He knows exactly which buttons to push, at just the right time, so that we will become angry with each other and be divisive.

Satan wants to destroy God's church. Let's take a look at two of his favorite strategies so that you can learn to recognize these telltale signs that Satan may be using you, or others, to stir up strife in your church or ministry.

Strategy #1:
Get Insecure People to Turn
Minor Offenses Into Major Offenses

The enemy often uses people with emotional wounds and scars to stir up trouble. These people do and say exactly what they "feel." They don't operate in self-control, nor do they ask God to help them get over the hurt, as a more secure or mature Christian would do. Instead, they allow Satan to magnify incidents in their minds and make them appear to be much more important than they really are. The devil wants to get these Christians to believe that people have plotted against them and are purposefully trying to hurt them.

Here's an example of how this strategy works. Let's say a woman is in a crowded shopping mall when she sees her pastor. He stops to say "hello" to her, but then tells her he's sorry, but he doesn't have time to talk. She feels hurt that he didn't greet her more warmly and that he cut off their conversation so quickly. As she dwells on her hurt, she thinks, "He doesn't like me. As a matter of fact, he was downright rude. He is rather cold emotionally for someone who is supposed to shepherd God's people." She begins to feel that the pastor was trying to get away from her. She begins to "remember" other times when she had felt the pastor was not very friendly with her—at least not as friendly as he is with other people.

The devil pounds at the woman's mind for days concerning this situation, and her anger at the pastor builds. Her family and friends can tell something is wrong with her, so they ask her about it. Although the Holy Spirit tries to tell her to keep her mouth shut, she relates the incident to them. Remember, they are only hearing her side of the story, which by now is very different from what actually happened.

The devil is a supreme strategist, and he works hard to get believers upset with each other because he knows that the Holy Spirit will only work in an atmosphere of peace.

Her opinions affect their opinions, and they gossip about the incident and begin to ask others in the congregation if they think the pastor is unfriendly. These people in turn begin watching the pastor and his attitude toward them (just as the Pharisees watched Jesus continually, hoping to catch Him in some wrong behavior).

The pastor senses that something is wrong. He feels "pressure" in the atmosphere at the church services, but he cannot put his finger on the cause because his actions were purely innocent. Perhaps he was not feeling good the day he saw the woman in the shopping mall. He may have been extra tired or preoccupied with financial pressure from the church building program. He could have been late for an appointment and only had time for a simple greeting. Unfortunately, the pastor has no idea that he has even offended the woman or that she has been busy spreading strife throughout the church.

If you think this example is a bit far-fetched, you are wrong. These incidents happen all the time in the kingdom. Probably more damage is done by the spirit of offense than by any other spirit. It is the believer's number one enemy. It opens the door for multitudes of deep, dangerous problems that few know how to deal with.

The Bible states plainly that we are to forgive those who hurt us—quickly, frequently, and freely. (We'll talk more about this in chapter 8.) Insecure people, like the woman in the above scenario, carry a root of rejection. They need a lot of outward assurance that they are accepted. They lack feelings of worth and value from within, so they crave it from outside sources. They need other people to affirm their acceptance through their actions and words. Of course, these Christians don't intend to cause trouble when they take offense; they only want to feel better about themselves.

I have encountered many Christians like this in my years of ministry, people who took offense because I did not pay enough attention to them. I remember one woman who was reportedly highly offended by me and felt I did not like her at all. When the story came to me, I was amazed. I liked this person, and as far as I knew, I was always friendly to her when I saw her. However, she was telling people that I did not pay the same attention to her as I did to other people. She said I often walked right past her without speaking. When I was told about a particular time when

I had supposedly snubbed her, the truth was that I had not seen her. I absolutely did not see her!

If you can relate to either of these women—if there are specific people whom you feel dislike you or are avoiding you—you need to learn to trust God to heal your emotional wounds. He is the only one who can help you begin to feel better about yourself. Your confidence needs to come from Him.

When I asked the Lord why He didn't just make sure that I saw the woman who was so offended when I didn't speak to her, He revealed to me that He had "hidden" her from me. He said, "She thinks that the thing she needs most in the world is for you to pay attention to her. But that is not what she needs. She needs to place her confidence in Me. When that is accomplished in her life, then I will allow her to have more attention from peers and people whom she admires."

God wants to work in our lives. In order to do so, He must open up some old wounds so He can clean them out. As long as our insecurities are being met by others, we will never get completely well. Each "fix" only prolongs our problem. It is like covering a major wound with only a small bandage. God wants to heal us, yet we keep putting bandages on the problem.

Insecurity is a poison that affects every area of a person's life. Healing may be a bit painful, but it's better than being emotionally handicapped all your life. We must learn to trust God for the attention He knows we need.

What, then, is a godly response when someone does not give us the attention we think we should have? Paul had this to say to the Galatian church regarding the strife problem in the church: "For the whole Law [concerning human relationships] is complied with in the one precept, You shall love your neighbor as [you do] yourself. But if you bite and devour one another [in partisan strife], be careful that you [and your whole fellowship] are not consumed by one another" (Gal. 5:14–15).

Probably more damage is done by the spirit of offense than by any other spirit.

Love your neighbor as yourself…do unto others as you would have them do unto you. Would you want someone to judge you harshly, show you no mercy, gossip about you, and spread strife in your church or organization? Of course you wouldn't! And neither would I.

When someone offends you, resist strife by responding with mercy and understanding. Give the person the benefit of the doubt. Remember that love always believes the best. (See 1 Corinthians 13:7.)

God's Word is clear. Be careful concerning the problem of strife. If permitted to stay, it will spread. And if it spreads—you and the whole church may be ruined by it.

The second strategy that the devil loves to employ is this:

Strategy #2:
Demolish Young Ministries
Before They Can Demolish Him

I know people who are not in ministry today because they took the devil's bait. Not only did they let strife in—they invited it. Let me tell you about two different examples of this that I observed firsthand.

The first incident occurred several years ago when I began to sense a "dead" feeling in our weekly meetings. The atmosphere felt heavy. Then I noticed that whenever I approached groups of people who had been talking, everything suddenly got silent. I had the strange feeling that I was intruding. People whom I had been close to for years suddenly seemed uncomfortable around me. I tried to brush off the feeling because I believed these people were my best friends.

Unseen walls kept being erected everywhere. One day, some of the people I normally ate lunch with no longer wanted to go to lunch with me. I also noticed that when I talked with others about something I wanted to do in the ministry or about something I believed God was speaking to me about, I would get silence and an uncomfortable feeling instead of the usual encouragement. It was as if everyone knew something I didn't know, and nobody wanted to tell me.

When the lid blew off, as it always does, relationships were ruined and people backslid in their personal relationships with God. I believe, quite possibly, great ministries were sidetracked by the enemy through the effective use of strife.

What had caused this devastation? A woman who had been practicing witchcraft for many years became involved in our church. She said she had finally realized that she was lost, and she was born again and filled with the Holy Spirit; she desired to get her life straightened out. Everyone was very happy for her. We all love to see people who were in deep bondage set free.

This woman got involved in several ministry areas quickly. She began attending the Bible college where I taught three times a week. She attended the weekly meetings at our home church. She joined an outreach ministry to the mentally handicapped and faithfully attended all the early morning prayer meetings at the church.

Everything about her looked right, but something felt wrong. When I say "felt" wrong, I am talking about spiritual feelings—not emotional ones. I had a check in my spirit about this woman. I could not get comfortable around her. I wanted to get away from her every time she came near.

One day, at a 6:00 a.m. prayer meeting, I walked by her and almost shuddered. I sensed within my spirit that she had been praying for me—and I did not want her to. I later discovered she was praying, but she was speaking for the kingdom of darkness and releasing curses, strife, and other forms of wickedness upon my ministry.

Confusion eventually engulfed the congregation. Accusations against people in leadership began flying everywhere. There were so many lies and gossip. It was hard to know whom to believe. People who had been attending the church for years left. Many of them held lay leadership positions.

I find it interesting that once the church fell into spiritual chaos, the supposed ex-witch disappeared. Satan had used her to spread his lies. He had launched a battle against people's thoughts. He had tempted some with judgment and criticism, and they took the bait. They were gossiping behind the scenes. Strife was spreading. An angry undercurrent was flowing, and many were swept away in the current.

It took months to repair the breaches in relationships, but eventually, things got back to normal. Today the church is flourishing, and God is blessing our ministry mightily. Not only did we survive the attack, but also we were made stronger through it. We learned a lesson that has kept us out of Satan's trap many times since. However, some of the individuals involved have stagnated and gone no further.

The other example of how the devil tries to destroy young ministries involves the church I mentioned in the beginning of this chapter. In this case, strife entered into the church through the pastor and his wife. They were very sensitive and became offended when members of the congregation felt that God was calling them to leave the church and go elsewhere. When the pastor or his wife happened to see people who had left their church, they were unfriendly to them.

This couple harbored unforgiveness in their hearts. They wanted to control the sheep—not lead them. If they wanted someone to get involved with a certain church program, but that person did not want to, they gave that person the "cold shoulder."

They corrected and ostracized me several times—once for teaching the Word. Dave and I had hosted a home meeting for two years prior to coming to this church, and we felt led to continue to do so after we joined the church. However, the pastor thought Dave should be teaching the home meeting, not me. Because we wanted to be obedient to the will of God, Dave tried to teach and I tried to be quiet. But it didn't work, and I began teaching again. I am called to teach, not Dave. No matter what people say or think, we need to do as God intends for us to do.

Another time, God put it on my heart to buy ten thousand tracts and organize a group of women to hand them out at shopping malls once a week. All the women were friends of mine, and I was going to pay for the tracts personally. My goal was to distribute all of them in six weeks. I thought we could hand them to people inside the mall and put them on car windshields in the parking lot until the ten thousand tracts were gone. It never occurred to me to get the pastor's permission to do this! Because I didn't, he chastised me, saying I would ruin my marriage if I did not submit to my husband. But Dave was not having a problem with me—the pastor was.

Still another time, the pastor corrected me for casting out devils. Finally, our name was removed from the church bulletin as an approved home for weekly home meetings. This kind of treatment happened to many other people in the church besides Dave and me. This pastor thought he was doing the right thing, but he was inviting strife into the church through his pride and insecurity.

Dave and I wanted to leave the church and go elsewhere, but God kept telling us not to leave with anger or unforgiveness in our hearts. We were young Christians at the time, but we knew better than to harbor hard feelings toward the pastor and other leaders in the church. Week after week we waited for God to release us. Week after week we watched the attendance decline.

Peace and unity are to be primary goals for the church.

One day I had a vision during my prayer time that I was attending a funeral. I did not understand everything in the vision, but I realized the funeral was for the church. It was dying. About one hundred people were left in the congregation when God finally released Dave and me to attend elsewhere. That number gradually dwindled to nothing, and the church had to close its doors. (This pastor's ministry was eventually redeemed, and he later went on to be used by God in other ministries.)

When I look back at that situation and at some of the people who were members of that church, I am amazed to realize how many have well-known, national ministries today. Many of the ministries were not even birthed yet—except in the heart of God. Others were in the infancy stage. I believe the devil wanted to destroy these ministries before they could destroy him.

Satan wants to attack and devour the young. He attacks the babies and toddlers in the kingdom because they do not know how to defend themselves. I am so thankful that God had someone praying for me. I may never know who it was, but I know someone's prayers were used to save us from the ravages of strife on more than one occasion.

Make Peace Your Aim

Peace and unity are to be primary goals for the church. We are even to help watch over one another. If we see a brother or sister in the Lord becoming angry or getting upset, we should help restore them to peace if possible. This may be one of the meanings of the biblical instruction to be "peacemakers."

Never forget that strife destroys. It destroys relationships on every level and in every part of our lives. If you can learn to recognize and deal with strife, you will stop a lot of intended destruction. In the next chapter we'll look at one last form of destruction due to strife—our physical health.

Chapter 4
Summary and Reflection

It is important to fellowship with other believers in Christ who are free from strife. The Bible says in Hebrews 12:14–15, "Strive to live in peace with everybody and pursue that consecration and holiness without which no one will [ever] see the Lord. Exercise foresight and be on the watch to look [after one another], to see that no one falls back from and fails to secure God's grace (His unmerited favor and spiritual blessing), in order that no root of resentment (rancor, bitterness, or hatred) shoots forth and causes trouble and bitter torment, and the many become contaminated and defiled by it."

1. The Bible says, "That enemy of yours, the devil, roams around like a lion roaring [in fierce hunger], seeking someone to seize upon and devour" (1 Pet. 5:8). According to this chapter, what are two of Satan's favorite strategies for destroying the church?

   _____

   _____

   _____

2. Has Satan ever used either of these strategies in a church you have been involved in? Describe what happened.

   _____

   _____

   _____

3. Have you ever felt offended by your pastor or someone in your church? How did the devil strategize to divide you from others

and others from you? What happened? What would have been a better way to handle your feeling of offense?

_____

_____

_____

4. Do you have a root of rejection in your life? Explain.

_____

_____

_____

5. Are you harboring deep-seated offenses in your heart against other Christians? Explain.

_____

_____

_____

6. Suppose you are a doctor, your church is the patient, and conflict and strife the disease. Write a prescription for your church using Galatians 5:14–15.

_____

_____

_____

_____

_____

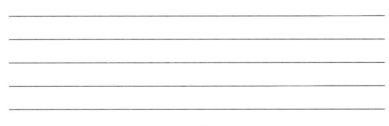

Dear Lord, I forgive everyone against whom I've harbored an offense. I ask You to forgive them for any sin they have committed against me and to restore my love and fellowship with them where possible. Strengthen

my insecurities, and help me to not be easily offended. Lord, I choose to walk as Christ did, loving freely and forgiving everyone. Give me a heart of love toward all my brothers and sisters in Christ, especially those who have mistreated me. In Jesus's name, amen.

five

A Headache and Back Trouble ... Again?

∞

I HAVE ALWAYS BEEN A VERY INTENSE PERSON. IN THE early years of our marriage, when I cleaned the house, I worked very hard, and if anyone made a mess after I'd finished the housework, I would get angry. I wanted a house to look at—not to live in. I knew how to work, but I did not know how to live in harmony with others.

Some people eat more when they are angry. It's a way to say, "I'll show you." Others eat to comfort themselves when they are hurting. I always lost my appetite when I was upset or angry. It's a good thing I did, or I would have been obese, because I was upset about something most of the time. I had strife with myself, Dave, the children, family members, neighbors, and even God.

When I got angry, I would stay that way for days or, occasionally, weeks at a time. I did a fair job of hiding my anger from those I wished to impress, but my inner life was almost always in turmoil. Being angry and upset seemed to make me more energetic for a while, but when the anger subsided, I felt as if someone had pulled the plug and drained all my energy.

Even though I felt sick most of the time, like most people I never connected my sick feelings to my anger. I had headaches, back trouble, colon trouble, and tension in my neck and shoulders. The doctor ran tests but could not find anything wrong with me; he concluded my physical problems were due to stress. This angered me even more! I knew that I was sick, and as far as I was concerned, it wasn't stress causing the illness.

But I was wrong. I didn't understand the link between strife and stress and how stress affects the body.

The Link Between Strife and Stress

How much stress can our bodies withhold? *Stress* can be defined as mental, emotional, or physical tension, strain, or distress. It was originally an engineering term. Engineers used it in reference to how much pressure or weight could be placed on the steel beams of a building structure without it collapsing. Today, more people are collapsing than buildings!

Thousands and thousands of people are sick, and I believe that a lot of our diseases are caused by *dis-ease*. Nothing is physically more stressful on our bodies than getting angry or upset—especially if we stay that way for very long. No wonder the Bible tells us, "When angry, do not sin; do not ever let your wrath (your exasperation, your fury or indignation) last until the sun goes down" (Eph. 4:26). The apostle James wrote, "Understand [this], my beloved brethren. Let every man be quick to hear [a ready listener], slow to speak, slow to take offense and to get angry" (James 1:19).

God created us for righteousness, peace, and joy. Our physical body was not meant to house strife, whether it be in the form of worry, fear, hatred, bitterness, resentment, unforgiveness, rage, anger, jealousy, or turmoil. While the body can endure a lot of punishment and still survive, it cannot withstand the day-after-day stress of living with negative emotions.

Our internal stress is often compounded by the stress we feel from living in a stressful, strife-filled world.

Life Often Adds to Our Stress

We can't live in this world and not experience some stress. God created our bodies to handle, and handle well, a normal amount of stress. But life itself seems to be becoming more stressful, particularly for people living in the United States, where everyone is in a hurry. The sad thing is that many people are going nowhere, and they don't know it. All of this creates a tense atmosphere that is supercharged with strife.

While the body can endure a lot of punishment and still survive, it cannot withstand the day-after-day stress of living with negative emotions.

Noise levels are growing at an alarming rate. Years ago you could pull up beside a car in traffic with its windows down and hear a restful or joyful song playing that would make you feel a little better. You might even exchange a smile or a wave of hello to someone even though you did not know the person.

Not so today. The music booming from cars is often so loud it can make you want to scream. If you smile or wave at someone, it may bring accusations of ulterior motives. If you look too long at someone, that person may scream obscenities at you.

Many families are also experiencing financial pressure. In many households, both parents have to work in order to pay the bills, or maybe the dad works two jobs. Many single mothers work two or three jobs, and when they go home at night, they still have to do all the work required to run a household. No wonder so many people complain that they are tired, worn out, and weary. Even those with only one job can get stressed and exhausted from doing their job.

Tired people succumb to temptation easier than those who are rested. They are more vulnerable to spiritual warfare—they are prone to stressful emotions like anger, frustration, and impatience. No wonder God established that we should work six days and then have a Sabbath—one day in seven to totally rest from all our labors. (See Exodus 20:8–10.) Even God rested from His labors after six days of creation work. (See Genesis 2:2.)

Our bodies can handle normal stress, but when things get out of balance or excessive, we often sacrifice our good health. When Dave and I were first starting our ministry, I experienced a lot of stress. I felt the weight of responsibility on my shoulders. I worried about the potential problems almost constantly. Where would the money come from? How could I get speaking engagements when nobody knew who I was? How could I get on radio stations? I lived in fear and human reasoning—I lived in stress.

While the stress I felt sometimes led to strife between Dave and me, I was mostly in strife with my circumstances. I could not seem to get things to move along as quickly as I wanted them to. I had a vision, and it was not progressing in my timing. I tried one thing first, and then another, but all to no avail.

Once again, I found myself in the doctor's office, complaining of backaches and headaches and other physical ailments. All the doctors I saw told me my physical problems were due to stress, but I knew God had called me to be in full-time ministry, so I didn't believe that my problems were caused by how I was handling my stressful job. Today I can see clearly that what the doctors told me was accurate. I may have been doing the job God had called me to do, but I hadn't learned how to do it peacefully so as not to create strife.

Tired people succumb to temptation easier than those who are rested.

Whether strife is the cause—or the result—of our stress, if left unchecked, it leads to illness. To understand why, it's helpful to be acquainted with the body's response to excessive stress.

Understanding the Body's Response to Too Much Stress

Let me share with you what your body goes through internally in response to this kind of stress. I am not a doctor, but I will try to explain what happens in my own terms.

Each time your emotions (worry, hatred, bitterness, and so on) rise to the boiling point, your internal organs have to work harder to accommodate the strain. When they begin to wear out, they will start showing signs of the strain they have been under.

The onset of stress sets off an alarm that tells your body to defend itself from a threatening event. Simply thinking of an upsetting or dangerous event can trigger the alarm. When this happens, your brain sends the alarm on to your adrenal gland, which releases hormones such as adrenaline, increasing your heart rate, raising your blood pressure, sending glucose to your muscles, and raising your level of cholesterol. The threat of stress sets in motion a complex chain of responses to prepare your body for "fight or flight"—either to attack what is threatening you or to run away from it.*

Your body says to your organs, "I am under attack! Help me fight this, or help me get away from it. I need extra strength and energy to help me in this emergency!" Your organs begin to help. They are equipped to handle emergencies. But if you live in a perpetual state of emergency, the time comes when the organs are exhausted from trying to handle all the emergencies, and they find they can no longer handle even normal stress. Suddenly, something snaps.

For a visual picture of this, take a rubber band and stretch it out as far as you can. Then, let it relax. Do this over and over. After a while, you will find that the rubber band loses its elasticity. It becomes limp. Keep the process up long enough, and finally, after one stretch too many, the rubber band snaps. Some-

---

* Archibald D. Hart, *The Hidden Link Between Adrenaline and Stress* (Dallas, TX: Word Books, 1986), 21–23.

thing similar happens to us if we keep stretching our bodies too far too many times. Sometimes the mind snaps; other times it's our emotions or physical health that snaps.

Stress causes illness by destroying the body's immune system so that the body can no longer fight off germs and infection. The organs just plain wear out, and the person "feels" exhausted.

Finally, sickness arrives. People say, "I don't know what's wrong, but I just don't feel well." They have headaches, backaches, neck and shoulder pain, stomach ulcers, colon problems, and other ailments. When they tell the doctor how they feel, they are told they have an "adrenal weakness" or a "virus" of one sort or another. In many instances the root cause of the illnesses is years of strife-filled, stressful living.

The good news is that Jesus did not leave us in a world that had the power to make us sick without giving us a solution. He said in John 16:33 (in my words), "I want you to have perfect peace and confidence. In the world you have tribulation and trials and distress and frustration; but be of good cheer, for I have overcome the world. [I have deprived it of power to harm you and have conquered it for you.]"

Live Positively

While negative thoughts, words, emotions, and relationships can cause stress—and stress can cause sickness—positive thoughts, words, emotions, and relationships can bring health and healing. Consider the following scriptures:

"A calm and undisturbed mind and heart are the life and health of the body, but envy, jealousy, and wrath are like rottenness of the bones" (Prov. 14:30). Emotional turmoil, such as anger, envy, and jealousy, eats away at good health and a sound body. A calm and peaceful mind ministers health to the entire being.

"My son, attend to my words; consent and submit to my sayings. Let them not depart from your sight; keep them in the center of your heart. For they are life to those who find them, healing and health to all their flesh" (Prov. 4:20–22). What brings and ministers healing and health? Meditating on God's Word and not on the things that cause stress. Jesus is our peace. He is also the living Word. When we abide in the Word, peace is abundant. It flows like a river.

"[Earnestly] remember the Sabbath day, to keep it holy (withdrawn from common employment and dedicated to God). Six days you shall labor and do all your work, but the seventh day is a Sabbath to the Lord your God; in it you shall not do any work, you, or your son, your daughter, your manservant, your maidservant, your domestic animals, or the sojourner within your gates" (Exod. 20:8–10). God told us to rest our bodies for a reason. He knows that when we take care of ourselves, our spirits will be more positive and we'll be better able to resist Satan's attempts to engage us in strife.

"Lean on, trust in, and be confident in the Lord with all your heart and mind and do not rely on your own insight or understanding. In all your ways know, recognize, and acknowledge Him, and He will direct and make straight and plain your paths. Be not wise in your own eyes; reverently fear and worship the Lord and turn [entirely] away from evil. It shall be health to your nerves and sinews, and marrow and moistening to your bones" (Prov. 3:5–8). I spent years reasoning and trying to figure everything out, and it affected my health adversely. But I have learned to cast my care upon God so that I don't live with the constant pressure. I feel much better physically now than I did when I was thirty-five. Why? Because I no longer worry.

Learning to trust God with my life has also prevented strife between Dave and me. In the past, I would keep pushing, trying to get Dave to see things my way. Now I back off and ask God to change what needs to be changed.

"A happy heart is good medicine and a cheerful mind works healing, but a broken spirit dries up the bone" (Prov. 17:22). How much plainer could it be said? A person who is happy, light-hearted, and cheerful will be healthy. An angry person is neither cheerful nor happy, and very likely not healthy either.

God's Word not only tells us that happiness leads to good health, but it also tells us how to experience happiness.

Happy Hearts, Healthy Bodies

Several years ago, when I was seeking to walk in peace, I was determined to find out how to enjoy a peaceful life. One day I came across this passage in 1 Peter: "For let him who wants to enjoy life and see good days [good—whether apparent or not] keep his tongue free from evil and his lips from guile (treachery, deceit). Let him turn away from wickedness and shun it, and let him do right. Let him search for peace (harmony; undisturbed-ness from fears, agitating passions, and moral conflicts) and seek it eagerly. [Do not merely desire peaceful relations with God, with your fellowmen, and with yourself, but pursue, go after them!]" (1 Pet. 3:10–11).

I still enjoy just reading over this passage and soaking up the power from its principles for successful daily living. It gives four specific principles for those who want to enjoy life—and protect their health.

1. Keep your tongue free from evil.

God's Word states clearly that the power of life and death is in the mouth. We can bring blessing or misery into our life with our words. Proverbs 12:18 says, "There are those who speak rashly, like the piercing of the sword, but the tongue of the wise brings healing." When we speak rashly, we often get into arguments. So choose your words carefully; have your mouth full of the Word of God, not your own words. Your health will improve!

2. Turn away from wickedness.

We must take action to remove ourselves from wickedness or from a wicked environment. The action we must take could mean altering our friendships and eating lunch alone instead of sitting in the middle of office gossip. It could even mean loneliness for a period of time. New beginnings require endings. The desire to have a new life—one filled with righteousness, peace, and joy—will require the death of some things as we wait on God to give birth to new ones.

3. Do right.

The decision to do right must follow the decision to stop doing wrong. It may appear that the one automatically follows the other, but it doesn't. Both are definite choices. Repentance is twofold; it requires turning away from sin and turning to righteousness. Some people turn from their sin, but they never make the decision to start doing right. As a result, they are lured back into sin.

The Bible is filled with the following "positive replacement principle": "Rejecting all falsity and being done now with it, let everyone express the truth with his neighbor. . . . Let the thief steal no more, but rather let him be industrious, making an honest living with his own hands" (Eph. 4:25, 28).

4. Search for peace.

Notice that we must search for it, pursue it, and go after it. We cannot merely desire peace without any accompanying action, but we must desire peace with action. We need to search for peace in our relationship with God, with ourselves, and with others.

How much plainer could it be said? A person who is happy, lighthearted, and cheerful will be healthy.

When I started living by these principles, not only did my relationships improve, but so did my health. Yours will, too.

As you seek to eliminate stress and strife from your life, remember that, "He who is in you is greater than he who is in the world" (1 John 4:4, NKJV).

Chapter 5
Summary and Reflection

∞

Stress was originally an engineering term used when determining how much pressure steel beams or other structural features could endure before they began to buckle and finally collapse. Unresolved anger and other forms of strife produce the same effect upon your body.

Here's what the Bible says about anger in Ephesians 4:26: "When angry, do not sin; do not ever let your wrath (your exasperation, your fury or indignation) last until the sun goes down." Then in the Book of James we read, "Understand [this], my beloved brethren. Let every man be quick to hear [a ready listener], slow to speak, slow to take offense and to get angry" (James 1:19).

1. Using Ephesians 4:26 and James 1:19, write a biblical response to our feelings of anger.

   _____

   _____

2. How have stress and strife affected your health in the past?

   _____

   _____

3. What factors are producing stress in your life right now? Consider the symptoms of strife listed in chapter 1 as well as your circumstances and relationships. How might they be affecting your health?

   _____

   _____

4. Do you often feel tired and worn out? God tells us to rest our bodies. (See Exodus 20:8–11.) Apply this principle to your situation. How might your situation change?

_____

_____

5. How can meditating on God's Word (Prov. 4:20–22) and learning to trust God with your life (Prov. 3:5–6) keep you free from stress-induced illnesses?

_____

_____

6. According to Proverbs 17:22, happiness and health are directly linked. First Peter 3:10–11 tells us the keys to enjoying life. Apply each of those keys to your situation. How might they reduce your level of stress?

Keep your tongue free from evil.

_____

_____

Turn away from wickedness.

_____

_____

Do right.

_____

_____

Search for peace.

_____

_____

Dear heavenly Father, please give me the grace I need to live in a stress-filled world. Help me to speak words that produce peace in my own mind and body and in the lives of others. Help me to never let the sun go down on my anger and to get the rest my body needs. I surrender my thoughts, words, attitudes, and health to You. Amen.

Part II

Healing Troubled Relationships

six

Trust God,
Not Self

∞

WHEN GOD TOLD ABRAM (WHOM HE LATER named Abraham) to take his household and move to another country, Abram took his nephew, Lot, and Lot's household with him (Gen. 12:1–4). When they finally settled in Bethel, they had so many animals, tents, and possessions that the land couldn't support both households. Not only that, but also their servants were quarreling. So Abram went to Lot and told him that they needed to separate so each could have enough land for their herds. In addition, Abram humbled himself and gave Lot the first choice of available land.

Here is what happened next: "And Lot looked and saw that everywhere the Jordan Valley was well watered. Before the Lord destroyed Sodom and Gomorrah, it was all like the garden of the Lord, like the land of Egypt, as you go to Zoar.

Then Lot chose for himself all the Jordan Valley and [he] traveled east. So they separated" (Gen. 13:10–11).

This was a potentially explosive predicament. Here was an opportunity for the strife that was already affecting their herdsmen to affect the relationship between Abram and Lot. However, Abram did not let that happen. Instead, he resisted strife by humbling himself (he denied his pride). Instead of trying to look after his own interests, he trusted God with his future.

Abram's generous offer diffused the volatility of the situation. After all, how could Lot become angry when Abram was being so loving and considerate? Of course, Lot chose the best piece of land—the well-watered, fertile Jordan valley. He selfishly took the best for himself and did not consider Abram. Look at the results: "Abram dwelt in the land of Canaan, and Lot dwelt in the cities of the [Jordan] Valley and moved his tent as far as Sodom and dwelt there. But the men of Sodom were wicked and exceedingly great sinners against the Lord" (Gen. 13:12–13).

Selfishness always leads to problems, and this was true for Lot. Sodom was such a wicked city that God decided to destroy it, but he told Lot that He would wait until Lot and his family were safely out of the city before doing so. Lot and his wife and two daughters had to flee so quickly, they must have taken very little of their cattle and possessions, if any, with them. But the loss of his wealth was only the beginning of Lot's problems. When his wife disobeyed God by looking back at Sodom as it burned, God turned her into a pillar of salt. But the worst calamity was that Lot ended up impregnating both of his daughters, who had on separate occasions encouraged their father to get so drunk that he was not even aware of it when each of them slept with him.

Lot selfishly tried to protect his own interests, and as a result he reaped a harvest of devastation and destruction.

Now let's see how Abram fared: "The Lord said to Abram after Lot had left him, Lift up now your eyes and look from the place where you are, northward and southward and eastward and westward; for all the land which you see I will give to you and to your posterity forever. And I will make your descendants like the dust of the earth, so that if a man could count the dust of the earth, then could your descendants also be counted. Arise, walk through the land, the length of it and the breadth of it, for I will give it to you" (Gen. 13:14–17).

Abram resisted strife and gave up his "rights" to the land in order to maintain peace between Lot and himself. The seed of obedience blossomed back to Abram in the harvest of God's promise to give him everything his eye could see.

This story teaches two powerful truths:

1. When we try to look after our own interests and keep God out of the solution, we fail miserably, often creating even more problems and strife.

2. When we trust God to take care of us, He will lavish His blessings upon us. He will prove faithful.

Let's examine each of these.

Self-Care Sows a Harvest of Destruction and Strife

If we choose to put our faith (trust and confidence) in ourselves, we will quickly learn that self-care does not produce supernatural results. For years I wore myself out mentally, emotionally, and physically with my efforts at self-care. Because of the physical and emotional abuse I endured as a child at the hands of people who should have taken care of me, and again during my first marriage, I thought I was the only person I could trust. I did not understand that my efforts at self-care were only adding to the problems in my relationships and life.

The Book of James clearly shows us how strife comes in through self-care: "What leads to strife (discord and feuds) and how do conflicts (quarrels and fightings) originate among you? Do they not arise from your sensual desires that are ever warring in your bodily members? You are jealous and covet [what others have] and your desires go unfulfilled; [so] you become murderers. [To hate is to murder as far as your hearts are concerned.] You burn with envy and anger and are not able to obtain [the gratification, the contentment, and the happiness that you seek], so you fight and war. You do not have, because you do not ask" (James 4:1–2).

Faith in self will always bring failure.

What happens when we try to "force" others to treat us right? It doesn't work! In fact, it often makes the situation even worse. This was true for Lot, and it was also true for a good friend of mine who was trying to change her husband.

The two of them seemed plagued with one disaster after another. My friend wore a frozen "charismatic" grin on her face all the time, so, from outward appearances, everything looked good. As I looked at her life from the outside, her problems and difficulties seemed unfair. I was tempted to pray: "God, why aren't You protecting her? She is so sweet and does so much for others. She tithes and is in church every time the doors open."

Finally, everything literally caved in on my friend—the roof of her house collapsed! Only then did she finally tell me what was really wrong. She said that she and her unsaved husband did not get along and were always in strife, mostly due to her efforts to try to change him. He was not a warring man. In fact, he was rather passive about everything, and his lack of interest in her, in their home, in their church, and in their life was a constant source of irritation to her. She had strife in her soul concerning her husband, and it came out through her judgmental attitude and her continual nagging and criticizing.

She told me that God had been talking with her about this, but she hadn't listened. She felt it was unreasonable for Him to ask her to be a peacemaker in her home when she felt the problem wasn't hers. She told the Lord that she just could not be quiet and let her husband get by with his irritating behavior.

My friend was operating in self-care. God would have taken care of her, but she was too busy trying to protect her own interests. She told me that she actually said to God: "I know what You are telling me, but I just cannot do it." Rather than trust God and humble herself to do what He was telling her to do, she chose to trust herself—and disaster ensued. Not only did she fail to change her husband, but she also invited destruction into their lives through her disobedience.

Faith in self will always bring failure. We are to "put no confidence...in the flesh" (Phil. 3:3). Not in our own flesh—or anyone else's.

However, when we enter into a relationship with God, we realize an awesome truth. God *wants* to take care of us. We can retire from self-care.

Trust in God Sows a Harvest of Blessing and Peace

When our circumstances seem out of control, or when others are hurting us or taking advantage of us, we naturally want to try to line things up in our favor. God wants to give us favor, and we must trust Him for it.

Like me, many people have difficulty trusting God because of past hurts. But God is not like other people. We can trust Him! Psalm 23:6 tells us, "Surely or only goodness, mercy, and unfailing love shall follow me all the days of my life."

How comforting it is to be assured of His special care: "Casting the whole of your care [all your anxieties, all your worries, all your concerns, once and for all] on Him, for He cares for you affectionately and cares about you watchfully" (1 Pet. 5:7). This is a wonderful verse!

Although God wants to take care of us, His hands are tied by our unbelief and works of the flesh. He is a gentleman and will not just take over without being invited to do so. He waits until we give up the job of self-care and place our trust and confidence in Him. The law of faith, mentioned in 1 Peter 5:7, is this: *when you stop trying to take care of yourself, you release God to take care of you!*

I have discovered that it is very hard to walk in obedience to God and in love with others if my primary interest is that "I" don't get hurt or taken advantage of. However, when I allow

God to be God in my life, He honors three distinct promises He makes in Psalm 91:15, which says, "He shall call upon Me, and I will answer him; I will be with him in trouble, I will deliver him and honor him."

According to this verse, when we trust God to take care of our concerns:

1. He will be with us in trouble.
2. He will deliver us.
3. He will honor us.

Honor is a place of lifting up. When God honors a believer, He lifts up or exalts that person. When we refuse to try and take care of ourselves, we are admitting that we need God's help. It is an act of humility, and that act of faith places us in the direct line of God's exaltation. Peter wrote, "Therefore humble yourselves [demote, lower yourselves in your own estimation] under the mighty hand of God, that in due time He may exalt you" (1 Pet. 5:6).

When we trust God, we are in line for a promotion. God will honor us and reward us as we place our faith in Him. The writer to the Hebrews said, "But without faith it is impossible to please and be satisfactory to Him. For whoever would come near to God must [necessarily] believe that God exists and that He is a rewarder of those who earnestly and diligently seek Him [out]" (Heb. 11:6).

When we exercise the faith to trust Him, our faith releases additional promises in the Word of God. Paul speaks of "a measure of faith" that is given to every person (Rom. 12:3, NKJV). We have faith as a gift from God. It grows and develops as we use it. We need supernatural results in our lives. The way to obtain them is by allowing God to be God.

Repeatedly, God's Word teaches that God is our defense, our vindicator, and our reward. (See Psalm 27:1; 59:9; Matthew 22:44.) He brings justice and recompense into our lives. (See Deuteronomy 32:35; Psalm 89:14.) He did for Abram. God gave Abram so many descendants that they could not be counted, and He gave him more land than he had before.

Rather than trying to make someone treat you fairly, pray for them, and trust God to take care of you.

In the world's system, you work hard and then get your reward. In God's economy, you trust Him deeply and then receive your reward. I am not suggesting that we live in passivity, but I am strongly urging that we avoid all works of the flesh. Living by the arm of the flesh invites strife—within ourselves, with God, and with others.

Consider the following scriptures. They will encourage you to retire from self-care and look for God's reward as you place your faith in Him.

"After these things, the word of the Lord came to Abram in a vision, saying, Fear not, Abram, I am your Shield, your abundant compensation, and your reward shall be exceedingly great" (Gen. 15:1).

"The Word of the Lord is perfect, His ordinances are true and right, by them we are warned (illuminated and instructed);

and in keeping them there is great reward" (Ps. 19:8–11, author's paraphrase).

"Men will say, Surely there is a reward for the [uncompromisingly] righteous; surely there is a God Who judges on the earth" (Ps. 58:11).

"For I will surely deliver you; and you will not fall by the sword, but your life will be [as your only booty and] as a reward of battle to you, because you have put your trust in Me, says the Lord" (Jer. 39:18).

"But when you pray, go into your [most] private room, and, closing the door, pray to your Father, Who is in secret; and your Father, Who sees in secret, will reward you in the open" (Matt. 6:6).

Rather than trying to make someone treat you fairly, pray for them, and trust God to take care of you. You may pray in secret, with a tearstained face, but God will reward you in the open.

When we trust in ourselves, it leads to strife. When we trust God, it leads to peace—peace within ourselves, peace with God, and peace with others.

Chapter 6
Summary and Reflection

Psalm 23 says, "The Lord is my Shepherd [to feed, guide, and shield me], I shall not lack. He makes me lie down in [fresh, tender] green pastures; He leads me beside the still and restful waters. He refreshes and restores my life (my self); He leads me in the paths of righteousness [uprightness and right standing with Him—not for my earning it, but] for His name's sake.

"Yes, though I walk through the [deep, sunless] valley of the shadow of death, I will fear or dread no evil, for You are with me; Your rod [to protect] and Your staff [to guide], they comfort me. You prepare a table before me in the presence of my enemies. You anoint my head with oil; my [brimming] cup runs over. Surely or only goodness, mercy, and unfailing love shall follow me all the days of my life, and through the length of my days the house of the Lord [and His presence] shall be my dwelling place."

God has made a commitment to us to take care of us.

1. According to Genesis 13:14–17, Abraham had a God-given right to enjoy the rich lands that Lot chose. Describe the possible motives of both Abram's and Lot's hearts.

_____

_____

2. What principles do you glean from Abram's actions with Lot that can help you with your own relationship problems?

_____

_____

3. Consider the concept of "self-care" for a moment. What does this mean for you? How have you chosen to take care of yourself rather than trust God to take care of you?

_____

_____

4. Trying to take care of ourselves is one of the main causes of problems in our relationships. Describe a situation in which your efforts at self-care fueled strife in one or more of your relationships.

_____

_____

5. Read the following scriptures, and then write God's personal promise to you in each of them.

   Psalm 27:1

   _____

   _____

   Psalm 59:9

   _____

   _____

   Matthew 22:44

   _____

   _____

   Deuteronomy 32:35

   _____

   _____

   _____

Psalm 89:14

_____

_____

6. Rather than trying to make someone treat you fairly, choose to pray for that person and leave his or her behavior to God. Write a personal commitment to leave the behavior of others in God's hands.

_____

_____

_____

_____

_____

Lord, show me how to diffuse potentially strife-filled situations. I give up my rights to You. Show me when being a peacemaker is more important than enjoying what is rightfully mine.

Release me from the strife-filled bondage of constantly struggling to make things happen for myself. Deliver me from the bondage of constantly feeling the need to protect myself. I choose to trust You to be a Good Shepherd who will care for me, watch over me, and protect me from harm at the hands of others. In Jesus's name, amen.

seven

Make Friends
With Yourself

∞

ARE YOU AT PEACE WITH YOURSELF? MOST PEOPLE are at war with themselves. Since we spend more time with ourselves than we do with anyone else, this can be a major problem. After all, we cannot get away from ourselves! To make matters worse, if we don't get along with ourselves, we probably can't get along with other people either. If we don't enjoy ourselves, we don't enjoy anyone.

This was true for me. I suffered from not liking myself for many years, but I didn't realize it. Nor did I understand that my self-rejection and self-hatred were why I didn't get along with most people and why most people could not get along with me. My relationships had a lot of strife because I was in strife with myself. People disliked me because I disliked myself.

The way we see ourselves is the way others will see us. We see this principle illustrated in Numbers 13, when the twelve spies Moses sent to investigate the Promised Land came back from their scouting expedition. Ten of the spies gave a very negative report: "There we saw the Nephilim [or giants], the sons of Anak, who come from the giants; *and we were in our own sight as grasshoppers, and so we were in their sight*" (Num. 13:33, emphasis added).

Because the ten spies saw themselves as "grasshoppers," their enemy saw them as grasshoppers, too. We reap what we sow. (See Galatians 6:7.) How can we expect others to accept us if we reject ourselves? How can we expect to make peace with others if we haven't made peace with ourselves?

Why People Reject Themselves

It would be easy to accept ourselves if we had no flaws. But we do have flaws. The number one reason most people reject themselves is because of their weaknesses and mistakes. They can't separate their "who" from their "do," and consequently they carry shame and reproach from the past. They focus so much on their faults that they can't see their strengths.

Recently, after attending one of our seminars, a woman told me, "I had so much strife in my life that there was not one area or relationship that was not strife filled and strife controlled." She went on to say that everything she did was motivated by and done with strife. She was continually disappointed with herself and judging and criticizing herself. She had contempt for all her faults and weaknesses, and she had never been able to see her strengths. Because she rejected herself, she rejected all the abilities God had given her. She felt terrible about who she was and was constantly striving to be better.

She said that she had heard people speak of "the peace that passes understanding," but she had never understood what they meant until she heard me teach on strife. When she learned that God didn't count her weaknesses and flaws against her, she experienced peace for the first time in her life.

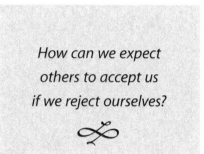

How can we expect others to accept us if we reject ourselves?

You see, we all have some strengths and some weaknesses. The apostle Paul testified: "I will all the more gladly glory in my weaknesses and infirmities, that the strength and power of Christ (the Messiah) may rest (yes, may pitch a tent over and dwell) upon me!" (2 Cor. 12:9).

Paul wrestled with his weaknesses, but he learned that Christ's strength and grace would be sufficient. If we want to learn to accept ourselves, this is essential for us to do as well. We need to know who we are, see our weaknesses as Jesus sees them, know where to lean, and beware of judging others—and beware of their judgments of us. Most of all, we need to live in the truth of our righteousness.

Know Who You Are

God's Word assures us that we have tremendous value because of who we are—God's beloved children. What I do is not always perfect. But I still know who I am—a child of God whom He loves very much. My worth and value come from the fact that Jesus died for me, not because I do everything perfectly. (See Romans 3:22–23; 4:5.)

You have tremendous worth and value. You are special to God, and He has a good plan for your life. (See Jeremiah 29:11.) You have been purchased with the blood of Christ. (See Acts 20:28.) The Bible refers to the "precious blood of Christ," indicating that Christ paid a high price indeed to ransom you and me (1 Pet. 1:19). Believe that you are God's beloved child. The truth will bring healing to your soul and freedom to your life.

Another step toward making friends with yourself is learning to see your weaknesses as Jesus sees them.

See Your Weaknesses as Jesus Sees Them

God's Word contains many examples of weak people through whom God chose to accomplish great things for His glory, including disciples. They were ordinary men who possessed weaknesses, just like you and me.

The Gospels clearly imply that Peter was a rugged and volatile fisherman who displayed impatience, anger, and rage. In one crucial moment, he was so fearful that he would be discovered to be a disciple of Jesus that he succumbed to a cowardly act—he denied that he even knew Jesus.

Andrew may have seemed softhearted and too kindly to be anything more than a follower. He avoided the role of leader, being willing to play "second fiddle" to his brother, Simon Peter, and his boisterous, competitive friends James and John.

James and John are remembered for little beyond the fact that their mother sought positions of equality for them at Jesus's side when He established His kingdom. Could it be they were a bit too ambitious?

Thomas was a man afraid to place his trust in his leader. Everything had to be proven to him before he could accept it.

And then there was Matthew. The religious leaders of the day were outraged that Jesus would even consider socializing with this lowly tax collector. Imagine their horror when Jesus dined with Matthew at his home and invited him to become one of His followers and close associates.

Probably the only man the religious leaders would have considered worthy of any admiration at all was Judas. To the world's eye, Judas had business strengths and personality qualities that spelled success. But his greatest natural strengths became his greatest weaknesses—and brought destruction into his life.

I find it interesting that those whom the world recommended, Jesus rejected. And those whom the world rejected, Jesus said, in essence, "Give them to Me. I don't care how many faults they have. If they will trust Me, I can do great and mighty things through them."

Jesus prayed all night before selecting the twelve men who became His close companions for three years. They had multiple weaknesses, and He knew it when He invited them into relationship with Him. Yet, with the exception of Judas Iscariot, they carried on ministry in a dynamic way after His death, resurrection, and ascension.

First Corinthians 1:25–29 unveils the heart of God toward those with weakness: "The foolish thing [that has its source in] God is wiser than men, and the weak thing [that springs] from God is stronger than men. For [simply] consider your own call, brethren; not many [of you were considered to be] wise according to human estimates and standards, not many influential and powerful, not many of high and noble birth. [No] for

God selected (deliberately chose) what in the world is foolish to put the wise to shame, and what the world calls weak to put the strong to shame. And God also selected (deliberately chose) what in the world is lowborn and insignificant and branded and treated with contempt, even the things that are nothing, that He might depose and bring to nothing the things that are, so that no mortal man should [have pretense for glorying and] boast in the presence of God."

Wow! These scriptures can give us such hope for the future. They tell us that God can use even me! And God can use you! We are equal in Christ, and so is every believer. Suppose one believer has a measure of 10 percent weakness and 90 percent strength, and another has 40 percent weakness and 60 percent strength. Most people would say the second believer is weaker than the first and, therefore, less desirable for any given task. But God does not see and judge as we do. Both of these individuals are equal to Christ, simply because He is willing to supply the added measure of strength to each individual. Thus, in Christ, they are both operating at the same level or capacity.

This is a marvelous biblical truth, and it sets us free to be all we can be—without fear of rejection and without having to fear our inherent weaknesses. If you grasp this truth, you will never need to be in strife with yourself again!

As I've said, I was at war with Joyce for many years. I did not like myself and tried to change myself continually. The more I struggled to change, the more frustrated I became, until the glorious day when I discovered Jesus accepted me just as I was. He, and only He, could get me to where I needed to be. No amount of struggle or self-effort could perfect the flaws in me. It is accomplished "'not by might nor by power, but by My Spirit,' says the Lord of hosts" (Zech. 4:6, NKJV).

So don't rate yourself as unusable just because you have some weaknesses. God gives each of us the opportunity to be one of His successes. His strength is made perfect in our weakness. (See 2 Corinthians 12:9.) Our weakness gives Him the opportunity to show His power and His glory.

Instead of wearing yourself out trying to get rid of your weakness, give it to Jesus. Get your eyes off what you think is wrong with you and look to Him. Draw strength from His boundless might. Let His strength fill up your weaknesses. You don't have to get your act together. You just have to know where to turn.

Know Where to Turn

For years I tried to fight my flaws and change myself, and I never made much progress. In my natural state, I tend to be harsh in my dealings with people—not a good trait in a minister. Yet I believed God had called me to minister on His behalf, and because He called me, He filled me with desire to do it. So, I tried to be gentle. I would determine, resolve, and exercise all the self-control I could muster.

Although I did improve, there were still those awful moments when the real me emerged. I am sure during those times people looked at me and said, "No way! God can't be calling you to do anything major for Him."

I wanted to believe God and to believe what my heart was telling me, but I heard the voices of people and let their opinions affect me. I also listened to the devil, who gave me a running daily inventory of all my flaws and inabilities. He reminded me how often I had tried to change and failed.

Then, after I had spent years wondering, "How can God ever use me? How can He trust me? What if I offend someone?" God finally showed me that my constant victory was dependent on my constant abiding in and leaning on Him: "Dwell in Me, and I will dwell in you. [Live in Me, and I will live in you.] Just as no branch can bear fruit of itself without abiding in (being vitally united to) the vine, neither can you bear fruit unless you abide in Me. I am the Vine; you are the branches. Whoever lives in Me and I in him bears much (abundant) fruit. However, apart from Me [cut off from vital union with Me] you can do nothing" (John 15:4–5).

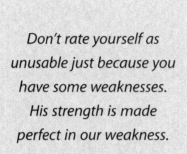

Don't rate yourself as unusable just because you have some weaknesses. His strength is made perfect in our weakness.

Knowing this truth forces me to lean on Him continually. My need drives me to seek His face. I cannot give Him glory unless I lean on Him. God does not need to lean on me—I need to lean on Him. Romans 7:24–25 says, "O unhappy and pitiable and wretched man that I am! Who will release and deliver me from [the shackles of] this body of death? O thank God! [He will!] through Jesus Christ (the Anointed One) our Lord!"

By God's grace, I finally came to believe that He chose me on purpose. I was not "pushed off on the Lord as a last resort" after He had tried to get two hundred others. He chose me! He deliberately chooses those the world would call weak and foolish, and He does it to confound the wise. (See 1 Corinthians 1:27.)

In addition to knowing who you are and seeing your weaknesses as Jesus sees them, if you want to make friends with yourself, you need to:

Beware of Judging Yourself—or Believing Others' Judgment of You

Are you in strife with yourself due to other people's judgments and opinions of you? Look at Paul's comment concerning the criticism of others: "But [as for me personally] it matters very little to me that I should be put on trial by you [on this point], and that you or any other human tribunal should investigate and question and cross-question me. I do not even put myself on trial and judge myself" (1 Cor. 4:3).

Some people were judging Paul's faithfulness. He did not try to defend himself, nor did he become angry. He simply said, "I do not care what you think. I do not even judge myself." Many times in the past I have opened to this passage and soaked it in, trusting the power of God's Word to deliver me from self-judgment and criticism.

We are not to pass judgment on each other or ourselves. Paul wrote to the Romans, "Who are you to pass judgment on and censure another's household servant? It is before his own master that he stands or falls. And he shall stand and be upheld, for the Master (the Lord) is mighty to support him and make him stand" (Rom. 14:4).

We stand because Jesus holds us up. When children learn to walk, their parents are always close by, holding their children's hands and helping them keep their balance so they will not fall and hurt themselves. We stand because our Father supports us and holds us up! We are upheld by His power, not our own!

If a neighbor came to my door complaining about the way my sons styled their hair, I would tell him (politely, I hope) to mind his own business. My children are not my neighbor's affair. This is the same protective attitude that our heavenly Father has over His children. Our flaws—and the flaws of others—are God's business, and God's alone.

Live in the Truth of Your Righteousness

Why is it so important that we get out of strife with ourselves? Because we cannot experience trouble-free relationships until we do. The kingdom of God is righteousness, peace, and joy in the Holy Ghost (Rom. 14:17). This kingdom principle contains a progression. If we desire joy, we must have peace, and to have peace we must have righteousness—a functioning reality of righteousness, not just a confession of righteousness.

> *We are righteous—not because we never make a mistake, but because Jesus never made one.*

God told Abram He had made him the father of many nations long before Abram had a child to be his heir. God spoke of it as if it already existed, and He has done the same about our righteousness. We can say we are the righteousness of God in Christ because the Word says that we are righteous (2 Cor. 5:21). The more we say this truth, the stronger the reality of it grows in us.

In order to move on to real peace, our righteousness must be established as truth in our soul. We must know that we know that we know. Our righteousness must be so established in our hearts that the "accuser of our brethren" (Rev. 12:10) cannot steal it from us with his lies.

We must be so established in our righteousness through the blood of Christ that even looking at our flaws does not defeat us. Abraham "did not weaken in faith when he considered the [utter] impotence of his own body, which was as good as dead because he was about a hundred years old, or [when he considered] the barrenness of Sarah's [deadened] womb" (Rom. 4:19).

You and I don't have to live in self-rejection and self-hatred any longer. *We are righteous*—not because we never make a mistake, but because Jesus never made one. He is the perfect one, and because of our faith in Him, we can count ourselves as righteous, too. God does! So stop striving with yourself and move into that blessed peace that leads to trouble-free relationships.

Chapter 7
Summary and Reflection

∞

First Corinthians 1:25–29 unveils the heart of God toward those with weaknesses: "The foolish thing [that has its source in] God is wiser than men, and the weak thing [that springs] from God is stronger than men. For [simply] consider your own call, brethren; not many [of you were considered to be] wise according to human estimates and standards, not many influential and powerful, not many of high and noble birth.

"[No] for God selected (deliberately chose) what in the world is foolish to put the wise to shame, and what the world calls weak to put the strong to shame. And God also selected (deliberately chose) what in the world is lowborn and insignificant and branded and treated with contempt, even the things that are nothing, that He might depose and bring to nothing the things that are, so that no mortal man should [have pretense for glorying and] boast in the presence of God."

1. Are you at peace with yourself? Do you accept yourself? What aspects of yourself have you struggled to accept?

   _____

   _____

2. Do you agree that the things we dislike in other people are often the things we dislike in ourselves? Explain your answer.

   _____

   _____

3. Write out a description of who you are, based on the truths found in Romans 3:22–23; 4:5; Jeremiah 29:11; Acts 20:28; and 1 Peter 1:19.

_____

_____

_____

_____

4. Have you struggled to believe that God could use you because of your past, your weaknesses, or what other people have said about you? Explain your answer.

_____

_____

_____

_____

5. How do 1 Corinthians 1:25–29, 2 Corinthians 12:9, and 1 Corinthians 4:3 apply to your situation? How can these scriptures give you hope?

_____

_____

_____

_____

6. We can say we are the righteousness of God in Christ because the Word says that we are righteous (2 Cor. 5:21). What can you do to establish this truth in your soul? How can you begin to live in this truth?

_____

_____

_____

_____

Dear Lord, I choose to accept myself as I am. I thank You for making me the person I am, with all my imperfections and flaws. Be my strength where I am weak, and give me the grace I need to accept myself the way You accept me. Thank You for loving me with supernatural love. Help me to see myself and my life through Your eyes. Amen.

eight

Make Forgiveness
a Lifestyle

∞

I LIVED FAR TOO LONG BEHIND WALLS I HAD BUILT to protect myself from emotional pain because I was determined not to give anyone a chance to hurt me a second time. If someone offended me, I cataloged it in my memory banks and put up a wall that kept that person at a distance or completely out of my life.

I was no longer being abused, but I held the abuse in my heart. It continued to cause pain in my life because I refused to trust God to vindicate me. It took many years for me to realize that I could not love anyone as long as I kept myself prisoner behind the walls of unforgiveness. I also had to learn that I really could not love and be loved until I was willing to take a chance on being hurt. Love hurts sometimes, but it also heals. It is the only force that will override

97

hatred, anger, and unforgiveness. It is the only force that can heal broken or troubled relationships.

The world is filled with hurt and hurting people, and my experience has been that hurting people hurt others. The devil works overtime among God's people to bring offense, strife, and disharmony, but we can override his attempts to sow hatred, bitterness, anger, and unforgiveness. We can be quick to forgive.

Forgiveness closes the door to Satan's attack so that he cannot gain a foothold that might eventually become a stronghold. It can prevent or end strife in our relationships with others. No wonder Scripture tells us over and over that we are to forgive those who hurt or offend us. Paul wrote, "Be gentle and forbearing with one another and, if one has a difference (a grievance or complaint) against another, readily pardoning each other; even as the Lord has [freely] forgiven you, so must you also [forgive]" (Col. 3:13).

Jesus made forgiveness a lifestyle, and He taught His disciples to do the same. Let's take a look at what He has to say about forgiveness in Matthew 18.

The Parable of the Ungrateful Servant

"Therefore the kingdom of heaven is like a human king who wished to settle accounts with his attendants. When he began the accounting, one was brought to him who owed him 10,000 talents [probably about $10,000,000], and because he could not pay, his master ordered him to be sold, with his wife and his children and everything that he possessed, and payment to be made. So the attendant fell on his knees, begging him, Have patience with me and I will pay you everything. And his master's heart was moved with compassion, and he released him and forgave him [cancelling] the debt.

"But that same attendant, as he went out, found one of his fellow attendants who owed him a hundred denarii [about twenty dollars]; and he caught him by the throat and said, Pay what you owe! So his fellow attendant fell down and begged him earnestly, Give me time, and I will pay you all! But he was unwilling, and he went out and had him put in prison till he should pay the debt" (Matt. 18:23–30).

The servant in this story owed so much to the king that he could never pay his debt. When he asked the king to forgive the debt, the merciful king did so. However, the same servant who was unable to pay his debt and who had asked for and received mercy was unwilling to give mercy to another servant in a similar situation.

The servant in this story represents us, and the king represents God. "All have sinned and fall short of the glory of God" (Rom. 3:23, NKJV). When we ask God to forgive us, through the sacrifice of Jesus, all of our debts are canceled. The Lord forgives our sins because He knows we could never pay Him what we owe. However, we are often like the ungrateful servant. We often refuse to release others from their offenses toward us, even though our heavenly Father has forgiven us. The parable goes on to teach what happens as a result.

"When his fellow attendants saw what had happened, they were greatly distressed, and they went and told everything that had taken place to their master. Then his master called him and said to him, You contemptible and wicked attendant! I forgave and cancelled all that [great] debt of yours because you begged me to. And should you not have had pity and mercy on your fellow attendant, as I had pity and mercy on you?

"And in wrath his master turned him over to the torturers (the jailers), till he should pay all that he owed. So also My heavenly Father will deal with every one of you if you do not freely forgive your brother from your heart his offenses" (Matt. 18:31–35).

When you and I refuse to forgive other people, we open a door for the devil to torment us. We lose our freedom—the glorious freedom that God intended us to have as we follow His ways. God is love. He is also merciful, kind, forgiving, and slow to anger. We often desire His power and blessings without wanting the lifestyle that goes with those things. Forgiveness must become a lifestyle. As soon as someone offends us, we must respond with forgiveness.

In fact, Jesus makes sure that we understand that we are not to put any limits on our forgiveness. Right before He tells the parable of the ungrateful servant, Peter asked Him an interesting question about how many times we should offer forgiveness.

How Many Times Do We Forgive Someone?

"Then Peter came up to Him and said, Lord, how many times may my brother sin against me and I forgive him and let it go? [As many as] up to seven times? Jesus answered him, I tell you, not up to seven times, but seventy times seven!" (Matt. 18:21–22).

I believe Peter asked this question because he was dealing with someone in his life who regularly offended him. This individual may or may not have been doing anything to provoke Peter;

perhaps one of the other disciples was simply a continual thorn in his flesh.

Peter thought that he should forgive a person up to seven times, but Jesus told him to forgive up to seventy times seven. Jesus was telling Peter to forgive whatever number of times it takes to remain in peace.

We are to forgive people who ask our forgiveness, even when we are not aware that they have wronged us, because our forgiveness frees them to be at peace. For example, at times people have asked me to forgive them for not liking me or for speaking unkindly about me. I wasn't even aware of their problem. It was not hurting me—it was hurting them. I gladly forgave them, because I wanted them to be free.

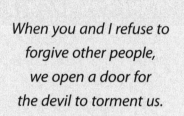

When you and I refuse to forgive other people, we open a door for the devil to torment us.

We are also to forgive people who do not ask our forgiveness, whether because they did not intend to offend us and do not know they did or because they are not repentant. Either way, forgiveness frees us from harboring bitterness and anger in our hearts. It releases us.

If you think you have offended someone, go the extra mile and simply say, "If I have offended you, I apologize." Then, if you discover that they indeed were offended, simply ask them to forgive you. The power of the words "Please forgive me" is amazing! Should the individual refuse to forgive you, at least you have done your part and can dwell in peace.

Not only can forgiveness heal our troubled relationships with other people, but it can also free us to enjoy the fullness of our relationship with God. You see, forgiveness as a lifestyle involves more than refusing to harbor anger and resentment toward other people; it also involves forgiving God when He doesn't do what we expect or want Him to do.

Many Christians are unknowingly angry with God. Are you one of them?

Are You Angry With God?

I was shocked when the Lord placed it upon my heart to minister to people in meetings along these lines. I didn't believe that many Christians were angry with God, but I was wrong. A hidden rift with God is a root cause of many emotional problems. It is the cause of bitterness and a sour attitude toward life that opens the door to every kind of misery and torment.

We were created to receive love from God, to enjoy and bask in it. We are to give love back to God lavishly, as well as to the world around us. God designed us for relationship with Himself— for warm, tender, loving, open fellowship. Anytime this is missing or hindered in any way, we will suffer.

The worst thing we can do when we encounter disappoint- ments and tragedies is to blame the trouble on God. God wants to help us! He is not the troublemaker—the devil is. It is the world, the flesh, and the devil that give us trouble—not God!

That is not to say that God will never lead us in a way that we would rather not go—because He does. The Israelites would have preferred a shorter route to the Promised Land. But God had a purpose in the way He led. Exodus 13:17–18 says, "When

Pharaoh let the people go, God led them not by way of the land of the Philistines, although that was nearer; for God said, Lest the people change their purpose when they see war and return to Egypt. But God led the people around by way of the wilderness toward the Red Sea. And the Israelites went up marshaled [in ranks] out of the land of Egypt."

God knows what is best for us. There are times when we feel, think, or desire a certain path. We are tempted to get angry with Him when He leads us a different way. When we feel disappointment with life, people, or with circumstances, it can develop into disappointment with God. This is

When we feel disappointment with life, people, or with circumstances, it can develop into disappointment with God. This is exactly what the devil wants!

exactly what the devil wants! If you are angry with God, bitter or resentful toward Him, He is giving you an opportunity as you read this book to be delivered from the trap that Satan has set for you. God is your helper—not your enemy.

From Anger to Trust

Perhaps you are wondering, "What about all the hard things that happen in our lives?" Many people ask this question because, with our finite minds, we cannot understand why God allows things like abuse, drugs, alcohol, war, natural disasters, and other things that usher in pain that is almost unbearable. We know that God can do anything He wants. We don't understand why He doesn't prevent the things that hurt us.

Many people who have been abused get mad at God. They cannot understand why He didn't help them. They believe they cannot trust Him. I understand how that could happen. Even though I was spared the torture of being mad at God for the abuse I suffered, I was still filled with questions. Why would a loving God sit by and watch a child suffer so terribly? Why didn't He stop the pain?

While God hasn't answered all of my questions, I draw comfort from this story.

A man who lost his son to cancer bitterly asked God, "Where were You when my son died?"

The Lord replied, "The same place I was when Mine died."

God didn't give a lengthy explanation, but His answer caused the man to close his mouth in humility. I feel the same. It is not my place to criticize God. Someday my questions will be answered. For now, I have peace of mind and heart because I put my trust in a loving God.

Sin and evil are in the world. The age-old battle between the forces of good and evil is still raging, and I suspect it will until the end of time. Even though it appears at times that evil has won over good, ultimate victory belongs to those who will put their trust in God.

There are many examples in the Word of God of men and women who did not understand what was happening to them. They went through periods of questioning, doubting, blaming, and even criticizing God. But they realized they were being foolish. They repented and turned back to trusting God instead of being angry with Him.

The psalmist is one of those people. Here is my paraphrase of his progression from anger to trust in Psalm 73: "God, it sure seems that the wicked prosper and do better than I do. I am trying to live a godly life, but it does not seem to be doing any good. It looks as if it's all in vain. I am having nothing but trouble, and when I try to understand it, the pain is too much for me. However, I have spent time with You, and I can understand that in the end the wicked come to ruin and destruction.

"My heart was grieved. I was bitter and in a state of upset. I was stupid, God, ignorant, and behaving like a beast. Now I see that You are continually with me. You hold my right hand. Whom do I have in heaven, God, but You? Who will help me? If You don't, there is no one on earth who can help me. You are my strength and my portion forever. It is good for me to trust in You, O Lord, and make You my refuge" (vv. 12–28).

If you are stuck in a place of bitterness toward God, I encourage you to go through the process of forgiveness. Anger toward God will stop us in our tracks and keep us from moving forward. It is a "spiritual roadblock"—perhaps stronger than any other. Why? Simply because anger closes the door to the only one who can help, heal, comfort, or restore our emotions, relationships, and lives.

While God doesn't need our forgiveness, we need to forgive Him in order to be released from bitterness and resentment. If we have been harboring a grudge against God, we must forgive Him. Only then can we experience God's power and blessing in our lives and in our relationships.

Forgiveness Stands Between Defeat and Victory

Forgiveness restores peace, but if we fail to forgive God when we need to do so, we will remain in strife. I saw this truth illustrated in the responses of two families I know who lost a loved one. The two stories are similar, but the endings are very different.

In the first situation, a woman lost her husband to cancer. During the time he suffered with his illness, he was born again, filled with God's Spirit, and became totally committed to the gospel. He made every effort to share his testimony with as many people as possible. He received prophecies that he would live and not die, and the entire family expected that God would heal him so that he could live his life as a testimony to the healing power of God. His family stood in faith and spoke the Word. They did everything they were told to do by their spiritual leaders or by doctors. Yet the man died.

Even though this woman felt confusion, anger, and disappointment, she was able to place her trust in God and come through victoriously. On the seventh anniversary of his death, I received a letter from her, thanking Dave and me for being with her during that time. She told me how much she loves the Lord today. He is her whole life. She enjoys serving Him in any way she can. She still misses her husband, but she is at peace and walks in victory.

Her children, however, have not fared so well. They kept some of the bitterness they felt when their father died. The confusion in their spirits has affected their spiritual progress. They have not turned away from God completely, but they did fall backward and have never recovered.

The second story involves another couple who had served God for many years and had several children. One of the children died suddenly, and the man became bitter toward God. I am sure his thoughts were something like this: "God, I have served You faithfully all these years, and I don't understand why You have let this happen. Why didn't You protect us? How could You let us down like this? We don't deserve this, God."

These kinds of thoughts continued until the man became so bitter and angry that it began to affect his life like a cancer. Eventually he divorced his wife and continued on in a life of sin—wanting nothing to do with God.

Unfortunate things may come into your life as well. You don't have control over every circumstance or offense that comes your way, but you can control your response.

Choose Forgiveness—Choose Life

God's Word says, "I have set before you life and death...choose life" (Deut. 30:19). When we encounter an offense or a circumstance that ushers death into our lives—physically, spiritually, or emotionally—the only sane solution is to choose life. If we don't choose life, death continues to spread until it steals our peace, joy, hope, health, and personal relationships.

Every time we are hurt, offended, disappointed, or even devastated—and there are many such times in our lives—we must choose how we will respond. Will we hold on to anger and resentment—and choose death? Or will we resist anger and offer forgiveness—and choose life?

If you have not been able to forgive the person who hurt you seriously, it may be because you have allowed the enemy to deceive you into believing that you can't forgive them. Make this affirmation daily: "I can and will forgive _____ for hurting me. I can do it because God's Spirit is in me and enables me to forgive."

Because my dad had sexually abused me for years, I spent a lot of time being angry and bitter toward him. My relationship with him was strained at best. But I gradually came to the realization that I had to make a choice to forgive him even though I knew it would be difficult.

With God's help, I was able to forgive my dad, and, in time, he was able to receive my forgiveness as well as God's. Before his death, I was able to lead him to accept Jesus as his Savior, and I had the privilege of baptizing him in water.

> *Make forgiveness a lifestyle by choosing to trust Him with the things you don't understand.*

Even though Satan stole what should have been a normal, loving relationship between a father and his daughter, God brought restoration and healing when I chose to forgive.

The church is filled with unbelieving believers. We call ourselves believers, but we don't believe we can do the things we know we should do. Take a more positive approach and be more aggressive against offense. Be quick to forgive. Be generous in forgiveness. Remember how much God forgives you daily. Make forgiveness a lifestyle by choosing to trust Him with the things you don't understand. Choose life.

Chapter 8
Summary and Reflection

Forgiveness is the fire extinguisher that douses the flames of strife that might otherwise consume our lives and destroy our relationships. Learning to forgive quickly is a key to battling strife. Paul writes, "Be gentle and forbearing with one another and, if one has a difference (a grievance or complaint) against another, readily pardoning each other; even as the Lord has [freely] forgiven you, so must you also [forgive]" (Col. 3:13).

1. Based on what you read in this chapter, why is forgiveness important? In what ways does it benefit us to forgive quickly?

   _____

   _____

2. Are there people in your life that you may need to forgive? Who are they, and what is their offense toward you? Keep in mind that if the thought of a particular person makes your blood boil, that is a good indication that you are harboring unforgiveness toward that person.

   _____

   _____

3. How would forgiving these people change your life and your relationships?

   _____

   _____

4. Although we may deny it, many of us are angry with God. We were created to receive love from God and to respond with our love to Him. Yet the root of many of our emotional problems stems from hidden or repressed anger toward God. This anger is also the cause of a bitter attitude toward life. Prayerfully ask the Holy Spirit to show you any hidden anger or hurt toward God you have buried deep inside. Write down what the Holy Spirit reveals to you about how you feel toward God.

_____

_____

_____

5. Every time we are hurt, offended, disappointed, or even devastated—and there are many such times in our lives—we must choose how we will respond. Write about a time when you chose to hold on to anger and resentment. In what ways was this a choice for "death"? Now write about a time when you chose forgiveness. In what ways was this a choice for life?

_____

_____

_____

_____

6. Can you give God your hurt, your anger, your disappointment, and your sense of betrayal toward others and toward Him? Will you choose to trust Him for His justice? Write a prayer turning your feelings and these relationships over to God and expressing your commitment to make forgiveness a lifestyle.

_____

_____

_____

_____

Dear Lord, I trust You for Your justice in my life. I choose right now to let go of my need to seek justice for myself. I forgive everyone who has offended me, including [speak out their names]. *I release them right now in the name of Jesus. I submit my life to You today, all over again. I don't understand all of the circumstances of my life, and perhaps I never will while I live on this earth. Lord, even though it is hard to choose to trust You at times, even though I do not fully understand, I submit my life to You. I thank You for loving me and keeping me until that day when I'll fully know as I am fully known—just as the Bible says in 1 Corinthians 13:12.*

nine

Disagree Agreeably and Magnify the Positive

∞

IT IS NOT EASY TO LEARN HOW TO AVOID CONFLICT AND have harmonious relationships. After all, some people are very difficult to get along with. Yet it is vital that we have peaceful relationships with all the people in our lives. God did not suggest that we avoid conflict—He commanded it: "And the servant of the Lord must not be quarrelsome (fighting and contending). Instead, he must be kindly to everyone and mild-tempered [preserving the bond of peace]; he must be a skilled and suitable teacher, patient and forbearing and willing to suffer wrong" (2 Tim. 2:24).

Everything God instructs us to do is for our good. When I remember that, it helps me follow through with obedience in difficult relationships.

One reason people have problems in their relationships is that they are not determined to resist strife. Or they resist it sometimes, but they are not willing to resist it all the time. Or they think that the only way to get along with another person is to become a doormat, so they never give an opinion or let others know how they are feeling when they disagree. Consequently they often end up angry and resentful.

I want to repeat myself to make sure that I have solidly made my point. *Staying out of strife is a continuing process in every relationship.* We must confront strife, get it out in the open and talk about it, and try to come to some terms of peace.

While it's certainly not easy to live in peace with others, I know from experience that it is possible. In this chapter I am going to share with you the following principles for how to resist strife and enjoy peaceful relationships with others.

- Learn to disagree agreeably.
- Magnify the positive.
- Accept each other as you are.

Let's take a look at each of these.

Learn to Disagree Agreeably

Lack of communication is the number one cause of many relationship problems, including divorce and even adultery. Many times people try to discuss things but immediately end up arguing because they disagree on something and don't know how to talk about it properly. Over a period of years, they stop trying to communicate, and major problems develop in their relationship.

Many of the challenges in Dave's and my marriage relationship had to do with our inability to communicate with each other in a godly way. We have very different personalities, and we often see things from two totally different angles. I am a strong, verbal person. Over the years, my mouth has gotten me into a lot of trouble because I always had to be in control so that no one could take advantage of me or push me around as my father had when I was growing up.

Staying out of strife is a continuing process in every relationship.

When we were first married, Dave was more passive than I was and less inclined to confront me. Then, after giving me some years to grow in God and partially overcome my past, the Holy Spirit began leading Dave to confront me more instead of just letting me have my way. I would get so upset that I felt like I wanted to run from the whole thing. Down deep inside I knew what God was trying to do; part of me sincerely wanted Him to do it, but another part of me (my flesh) wanted to scream and run.

When the Lord began teaching me about living in agreement, I could not understand how you could agree with someone with whom you had differing opinions. Just keeping my mouth shut did not seem to be an option for me. The devil told me over and over, "If you do this, you will become a doormat for everyone in the world to walk on."

When I first studied the scriptures on submission and how a wife should submit and adapt to her husband, it was almost more than I could take. Then, when I finally grew to the point in my walk with God that I wanted to be submissive to Dave, my initial response was to go to the opposite extreme. While previously I had something to say about everything, I started to feel I couldn't say anything at all. If Dave disagreed with me about something, I felt that "submission" meant that I could verbalize no further opinion. Otherwise, I would be in rebellion toward my husband.

This might not be a huge problem if you happen to be married to someone with whom you agree most of the time, but that was not the case with Dave and me. While I would keep quiet outwardly, it was eating away at me inside. I was being quiet, but I was still angry. I could manage to stay quiet for a short period of time, but then I would explode.

Dave continued to press on and confront me, and when we sat down to talk about our problem, we realized that a lot of our conflict was due to communication problems. I realized that *communication happens when all parties can express their hearts in a godly way, even when they disagree.*

We both had things to learn about how to properly communicate with each other. Dave had not confronted me for years, and when he started to do so, he came on too strong. I was not accustomed to being confronted at all, so naturally I overreacted and got upset every time he tried to share anything at all with me. I also had to learn to stop trying to manipulate him. If he disagreed with me on a matter, I would try to get him to see things my way. Dave could see my manipulation, and he started saying, "Stop trying to convince me, Joyce. If I am wrong, let God convince me. If you are wrong, I will let God convince you."

We needed balance, and we needed to learn how to disagree agreeably. Here is what we've learned about how to disagree agreeably:

- **Show each other respect.** Showing respect in our attitudes, voice tones, facial expressions, and body language has been the key for us in learning how to disagree agreeably. If I let out a huge sigh when Dave is trying to share something with me, it is obvious to him that I consider what he is saying to have little value. It says, "I have already made up my mind, and I am really not interested in hearing what you have to say." Most people do not mind if you have a different opinion than they do as long as you don't make them feel as if their opinion is ridiculous and of no value. There is a wise way to talk to people and a way that is not wise.

- **Drop it for awhile.** If we still disagree after allowing each other to say what he or she thinks or feels, we stop talking and wait to see what God does.

- **Be patient.** You may notice that I keep saying, "I learned," "We learned," "I am learning," or "We are learning." Being a peacemaker is a decision, and then it is a learning process. Don't get discouraged when you decide to abstain from conflict and strife and then, occasionally, fall back into old ways. Just be determined to learn. The Holy Spirit is your personal teacher. Each relationship is different, and the Holy Spirit will walk you through your unique situation as you trust Him.

I erected many walls that I didn't even know were there. Many of my reactions were based on old situations. Dave had nothing to do with the hurts from my past, but my perception was affected by the years of abuse and control. I still had many issues that needed to be dealt with in order for me to enjoy total freedom. They obviously do not get dealt with all at one time. The Holy Spirit leads us as He sees best. We will cross the finish line in victory if we stick with the program.

- **Search for an answer both parties can be satisfied with.** Let me give you a specific example. When Dave and I shop for household furniture, we often like two different things. Some men are not at all interested in helping to decorate their homes, but Dave has very definite opinions about what he likes. So do I. But our decorating tastes are very different. When we tried to shop for furniture, we were arguing by the time we had been in the first store for twenty minutes. By the time we got home, I was exhausted.

  Finally, I realized that my opinion is no more right than my husband's. Therefore we agreed to continue shopping until we found something we both liked. Many times one or the other of us had to give up the things we wanted so that we could find something we could both enjoy. At times we gave up, went home, and tried again another day.

- **Give in regularly.** Walking in love means giving up the right to be right. Dave and I both "give in" regularly—in a balanced way. In other words, I don't get my way all the time, and neither does he. We both are willing to follow the prompting of the Holy Spirit as to who needs to back off this time.

This isn't easy because, like everyone, Dave and I are each born with a generous portion of selfishness. We naturally seek what is best for ourselves, not what is best for the other person. Giving in requires humility. To do so with a good attitude is a sign of maturity. If I give in and let Dave have his way, but then spend the day feeling sorry for myself, what advantage have I gained? None at all!

There have been times when God led me to apologize to Dave when there was friction between us, but I refused because I had apologized last. I was willing to take my turn, but not willing to let go of legalism. I wanted to make sure I was not taken advantage of, and, therefore, I kept mental lists of who got his way last. I had to learn not to keep a literal record of who gave in last.

If two people are willing to take turns giving in to the other, it will benefit the relationship.

You will have to learn your own ways of disagreeing agreeably, because all situations are unique. All people are unique. If you are a believer in a relationship with an unbeliever, God may require you to give in more frequently simply because you have enough of the Word of God in your heart to enable you to do so. People who have no knowledge of the Word of God are led by feelings and thoughts. People grounded in the Word of God know that feelings and thoughts will lead to disaster.

Another way to enjoy harmonious relationships is to learn to focus on a person's strengths rather than on his or her weaknesses. In fact, if more couples learned to do this, there would be far fewer divorces.

Magnify the Positive

I love my husband very much. But for years I kept mental lists of every fault he ever displayed. I was a very negative person, and I searched for the faults and negative traits in people. I felt so bad about myself that I tried to find plenty of things wrong with others in order to help myself feel better.

One of the faults I found in Dave was that he played golf every Saturday. I thought he was extremely selfish not to realize how hard it was for me to be home all week with the children, with no opportunity to go anyplace. We had only one car, and he drove it to work.

I felt trapped within the bounds of the three-block radius in which I was able to walk. However, within those three blocks were a bakery, a grocery store, a beauty salon, and a dime store (as they were called then). I was not spiritually intelligent enough to realize that God had blessed me with the convenience of having all those places available within walking distance.

I never considered that Dave worked all week, had loved sports all his life, and that playing golf on Saturday was very important to him. I tried to get him to quit. I was angry almost every Saturday, which only made him want to play more. I tried to put him under "law," and it made him want to stay away all the more. The standards of the law only increase our problems; they cannot solve them.

I also complained that Dave did not talk to me enough, that he goofed around too much and wasn't serious enough, and that he wasn't aggressive enough. The list I kept of his faults went on and on.

In short, I hunted up everything negative and overlooked all his positive characteristics. I was so busy meditating on his faults and trying to correct them that I did not even realize what a blessing I had in my life.

> *When we verbally magnify people's strengths, we edify and encourage them.*

When God finally taught me—after many years of misery—to magnify the good in life and people, it was amazing how many great qualities I discovered in my husband! Of course, those qualities were there all the time. I could have been enjoying him all those years.

I discovered Dave is flexible and adaptable. He is very easy to get along with. He is not demanding at all. He is willing to eat almost anything. It does not matter to him if I feed him cold sandwiches or a hot meal. He allows me to buy anything for which we have enough money. Anytime I want to invite people over to the house, it is fine with him. If I want to go out to dinner, that is fine. I can choose the restaurant.

Dave also takes good care of himself physically. He looks much the same as he did when we married, except older. The list of his good points is lengthy—longer than the list I kept of his negative qualities.

Are you majoring in someone's faults when you could be magnifying that person's good points? Be positive about the people with whom you have relationships. If we sow mercy, we will reap mercy (Matt. 5:7). Do you want mercy applied to your weaknesses and faults? If so, be plenteous in mercy.

We all have faults, and if magnified, those faults become bigger than they really are. But when we magnify the good points in people, they become larger than the things that irritate us.

Today, if someone were to ask me what my husband's faults were, I would have to think hard to come up with some. Nobody is perfect, and Dave has some faults, but I don't pay much attention to them any longer, making them hard to remember.

I make an effort not only to think about Dave's strengths, but also to compliment him about them. When we verbally magnify people's strengths, we edify and encourage them. We are helping them be the best they can be. We pull the best out of them by magnifying the best.

Paul did this on a regular basis when he wrote to the various churches. Even when he corrected them, he also commended them for what they were doing right. He knew the art of correcting people without offending them. He expected the best of them, and in this way he inspired them to live that way.

We see an example of how he did this in the way he encouraged the Corinthian church to give. In his letter to them, he wrote: "Now about the offering that is [to be made] for the saints (God's people in Jerusalem), it is quite superfluous that I should write you; for I am well acquainted with your willingness (your readiness and your eagerness to promote it) and I have proudly told about you to the people of Macedonia, saying that Achaia (most of Greece) has been prepared since last year for this contribution; and [consequently] your enthusiasm has stimulated the majority of them.

"Still, I am sending the brethren [on to you], lest our pride in you should be made an empty boast in this particular case, and so that you may be all ready, as I told them you would be; lest, if [any] Macedonians should come with me and find you unprepared [for this generosity], we, to say nothing of yourselves, be humiliated for our being so confident. That is why I thought it necessary to urge these brethren to go to you before I do and make arrangements in advance for this bountiful, promised gift of yours, so that it may be ready, not as an extortion [wrung out of you] but as a generous and willing gift" (2 Cor. 9:1–5).

Paul encouraged the Corinthian church without sounding as if he was accusing or doubting them. He told them that he knew they were ready to give and had been for a long time. He says he is proud of them and that they will be a witness to other people. He gives them quite a buildup before he tells them that he is sending someone to make sure their offering is prepared as planned.

What a difference it makes in our relationships when we magnify and bring out the positive in people. It not only helps the other people improve, but it also helps us enjoy them more, right where they are.

So will this next point.

Accept Each Other as You Are

Another area of conflict for Dave and me had to do with our ministry. Dave often felt I was "running out ahead of God." I told him that his ministry was "waiting on God." Of course, I said this with sarcasm and disrespectful body language. Once I thought

I had heard from God about something, I wanted to go for it! Dave wanted to wait a while and make sure it was God.

A couple of years ago Dave had a vision of what he and I were like back then. He saw me as a team of wild horses, and he held the reins, trying to hold me back and give me some direction. He was not trying to prevent me from fulfilling the calling on my life, but he did not want me to get in trouble.

We were both wrong. I moved too quickly at times, and he moved too slowly. This is exactly why we need each other. God often puts us with people who are not like us so we can serve as a balance for one another.

Dave and I also had lots of quarrels around sports. He loved all kinds of sports, and I didn't enjoy any of them. His love for sports, and my lack of love for them, caused a great deal of disagreement in our household.

One day in the midst of a verbal squabble, Dave looked at me and said, "Joyce, I am doing the best I know how to do."

"Well, so am I," I responded.

We were finally just plain tired of picking on each other all the time and bickering. We actually shook hands. "Dave," I said, "I want you to know that I accept you today just the way you are. I believe that you are doing the best you can."

"Joyce, I accept you today the way you are," Dave replied. "I believe you are doing the best you can, too."

That was a new beginning for us! We finally started allowing each other freedom to be who we are.

People need freedom in order to grow. But God can't change a person if we stand in His way. God could not speak to Dave because I was too busy speaking to him. God could not change him because I was trying to change him. God needed my faith, not my help. Set the people in your life free, and trust God to make whatever changes are necessary.

We should do everything we possibly can to make a relationship work, especially in marriage. But what do you do if someone absolutely does not want to be in relationship with you?

What If You Just Can't Get Along?

We know from Scripture that God hates divorce. (See Malachi 2:14–16.) Husbands and wives are to be united—not separated. And yet, look at these verses in 1 Corinthians: "And if any woman has an unbelieving husband and he consents to live with her, she should not leave or divorce him. For the unbelieving husband is set apart (separated, withdrawn from heathen contamination, and affiliated with the Christian people) by union with his consecrated (set-apart) wife, and the unbelieving wife is set apart and separated through union with her consecrated husband. Otherwise your children would be unclean (unblessed heathen, outside the Christian covenant), but as it is they are prepared for God [pure and clean]. But if the unbelieving partner [actually] leaves, let him do so; in such [cases the remaining] brother or sister is not morally bound. But God has called us to peace" (1 Cor. 7:13–15).

I think this is a startling statement. We know that the Lord does not desire for any marriage to end in divorce. Yet Paul, speaking with inspiration from God, says that if the unbelieving partner does not want the relationship, and he or she leaves, let that person go because it is very important that we live in peace. Trying to force someone to stay in a marriage, when that person really doesn't want to, will only bring more tension and strife into the relationship.

I want to be very clear. I am not advocating that married couples separate if they find it difficult to get along with each other. The 1 Corinthians 7 passage says that if the "unbeliever" wants to leave the marriage, we should let him or her.

On the other hand, in some troubled relationships a time of separation might be necessary, particularly if the relationship is with a friend or a ministry or business partner rather than a spouse. When Paul and Barnabas faced some difficulties in their ministry relationship, they decided to go their separate ways in order to keep peace between them. Here is what happened:

"And after some time Paul said to Barnabas, Come, let us go back and again visit and help and minister to the brethren in every town where we made known the message of the Lord, and see how they are getting along.

"Now Barnabas wanted to take with them John called Mark [his near relative]. But Paul did not think it best to have along with them the one who had quit and deserted them in Pamphylia and had not gone on with them to the work. And there followed a sharp disagreement between them, so that they separated from each other, and Barnabas took Mark with him and sailed away to Cyprus.

"But Paul selected Silas and set out, being commended by the brethren to the grace (the favor and mercy) of the Lord. And he passed through Syria and Cilicia, establishing and strengthening the churches" (Acts 15:36–41).

Paul and Barnabas were experiencing the same troubles in their relationship that people experience today. Barnabas wanted to give his relative Mark a job. Paul had already had an experience with Mark and felt it would not be wise. A "sharp" disagreement arose between them (v. 39).

Apparently, it was so sharp they knew they needed to get away from each other. It would have been much better if they could have resolved their differences and continued to work together, but since that was impossible, the next best thing to do was to go their separate ways. We may need to do the same if we aren't able to work out our differences with close friends or ministry or business associates.

And what if you are married to another Christian and have tried all you know to do to work things out, and yet you still can't get along with each other? A time of separation is more desirable than a divorce. Perhaps during the separation both parties can see things more clearly. This frequently happens. People have time to clear their heads, let heated emotions cool down, and get quiet enough to hear from the Lord. They have time to ask God what He wants them to do in their situation.

In fact, many Christians believe that something like this happened with Paul and Barnabas. Paul certainly did mend fences with John Mark (the cause of his dispute with Barnabas), because Paul asks Luke to bring

Being a peacemaker is a decision.

Mark along toward the very end of Paul's life (2 Tim. 4:11). If Paul mended fences with John Mark, perhaps he had already mended fences with Barnabas.

Sometimes we stare at a person's faults so long that we no longer can see that individual's strengths. A time away from someone, even spending a week at a relative's house in another state, can help us see the good things about a person that we miss when he or she is always present. You know the old saying, "You never know what you have until you lose it."

The Bottom Line

Jesus is the King of peace. He said in Matthew 5:9, "Blessed (enjoying enviable happiness, spiritually prosperous—with life-joy and satisfaction in God's favor and salvation, regardless of their outward conditions) are the makers and maintainers of peace, for they shall be called the sons of God!" You may be more familiar with the New King James Version: "Blessed are the peacemakers, for they shall be called sons of God."

Being a peacemaker is a decision. If we are going to enjoy His blessings, we must decide to live in peace with others. We must learn how to disagree agreeably, magnify the positive, and accept each other. As we'll see in the next chapter, this last point is even more important when it comes to how we relate to our children.

Chapter 9
Summary and Reflection

Walking in peace with others is often challenging. If possible, the devil will try to undermine every one of your relationships with strife. You cannot always avoid strife. Sometimes you must confront it, get it out in the open, and try to come to some terms of peace.

The apostle Paul makes a powerful statement in 1 Corinthians 7:15: "God has called us to peace." If peace is God's will for our lives, He can heal our relationships and make peace possible.

1. List the relationships in your life that have been attacked by conflict and strife.

_____

_____

_____

2. It's possible that you are to blame—at least partially—for the problems in some of your relationships. However, it is also possible that you are being victimized by someone else's strife. Think carefully and prayerfully about the causes of strife in these relationships. Write down the hard-to-face truth you've discovered.

_____

_____

_____

3. Think about a recent disagreement you had with someone. Then prayerfully consider the principles for how to disagree

agreeably, which are listed below. Which of these principles could you have applied in that situation in order to keep peace with the other person? Explain.

Show each other respect.

_____

_____

Drop it for a while.

_____

_____

Be patient.

_____

_____

Search for an answer both parties can be satisfied with.

_____

_____

Give in regularly.

_____

_____

4. Magnifying the positive characteristics in a person is a good way to build relationship bridges. List some of the positive characteristics of a person with whom you've experienced strife.

_____

_____

5. Describe a situation when you felt responsible for changing the opinions of another. What was the outcome? Now suppose you were able to rewrite history. Describe the situation you just

mentioned, only change the details to respect and honor the other individual's opinion, while still remaining true to your own feelings and opinions.

_____

_____

_____

6. Sometimes we look at a person's faults for so long that we no longer see his or her strengths. Is there a (nonmarital) relationship in your life that is at a similar breaking point? Spend time in prayer asking the Holy Spirit to give you insight on how to handle the division. Write how you sense God is leading you to deal with this situation.

_____

_____

_____

Dear Lord, I commit to allowing others the freedom to hold their own opinions and to make their own choices. I trust You to mold and shape others into the people You want them to be. Help me to be a peacemaker in my attitudes, body language, and facial expressions. Please give me the grace to be gracious and positive in all my relationships. If some of my relationships are at the breaking point, show me how I might gain fresh perspective about the people involved. Help me to see the positive in everyone around me, and help me to speak in a positive manner, even when I must bring correction. Thank You, Lord.

ten

Accept Your Kids
for Who They Are

∞

I LEARNED THE HARD WAY THAT IN ORDER FOR PARENTS to have harmonious and positive relationships with their children, it is absolutely critical that we accept them for who they are and that we don't try to change them.

Dave and I have four children. Two I found easy to parent; the other two I found to be quite a struggle. While you might think it would be easy to get along with a child who is just like you, I know from experience that it can be just as difficult as getting along with a child who is very different from you. Many parents who have one child who is exactly like them often see in that child all the weaknesses they dislike about themselves. This was the case for my oldest son and me. I also had numerous struggles with my oldest daughter. However, she is my opposite in some ways, and I judged her for the weaknesses she had that I did not share.

If we parents want to have harmonious relationships with our children, we must be able to make a distinction between their weaknesses and their personality. Otherwise we may end up rejecting our own children, which breeds rebellion and all kinds of strife.

I didn't always understand this, and I tried my best to change things about both of these children. It didn't work. In fact, it only made matters worse and drove one of them away from me for a time.

Let me tell you what I did to stir up strife in the hearts of my children—as well as what I did later to resist it and bring healing—in the hope that it will help you avoid making the same mistakes with your kids. If you are already experiencing the pain of a damaging relationship, I hope this chapter will inspire you to make the decision to offer your child the forgiveness and love they need from you.

Learning to Accept David

Since my son David and I both have strong, "take charge" personalities, we were each trying to "take charge" of each other. I wanted him to do what I wanted him to do. He wanted to do what he wanted to do. And he wanted me to do what he wanted me to do. Even as a toddler, he would insist that I sit and play with him because he did not want to play by himself. I always felt, in some vague way, that my David was trying to control me. As he grew older, the problem only increased. I continually felt a struggle between us and really never understood what was going on.

I loved my son, but to be honest, I did not like him, and I felt terribly guilty about it. I know that many of the people who read this book have experienced the same thing. We know we should love and accept our own child. When that seems to be impossible, guilt begins to accuse. I realized later that the reason I disliked David had more to do with me, not him. I did not like myself, so of course I didn't like him either, since he was so much like me.

Although I have a strong personality myself, I did not enjoy being around anyone else who had one. I wanted to be in control—not to be controlled. If I had understood this when David was young, I could have helped him learn to be strong in a positive way. But since I didn't understand, I only added to the weaknesses in his temperament. He and I lived in continual strife, and it placed as much pressure on him as it did me.

Children can sense when a parent is not happy with them. David knew down deep inside that I was not pleased with him, and he felt rejected. I was not giving him the liberty to be who he was. As I did with so many people, I was trying to change him into what I would have liked him to be.

The Book of Proverbs warns parents about this very thing: "Train up a child in the way he should go [and in keeping with his individual gift or bent], and when he is old he will not depart from it" (Prov. 22:6).

I have learned a lot from the Amplified Bible translation of that verse. It does not say, "Train up a child in the way you would like him to go." It states that we should train our children according to their own individual gifts or bents—according to the "spiritual markings" we see on our children.

Had I been more spiritually in tune, I would have recognized that God had built David for leadership and that He had given my son the temperament to go with it. Instead of seeing that, all I saw was that David made me uncomfortable, and I wanted him to change.

David and I had serious problems in our relationship for a long time. But the more I learned from God's Word, the more I realized I was not handling the situation correctly. I vividly recall when our relationship began to turn around.

David was eighteen. One day God told me that I needed to forgive my son for not meeting *my* expectations. He told me that I was angry with David because he was not what *I* wanted him to be; He said that I needed to forgive him for this and to verbally accept him. I needed to let David know that even though I did not agree with all of his ways, I loved him and was willing to accept him as he was.

After I forgave David and told him that I loved and accepted him, our relationship began to heal and change. Not long after that, God called him to go to Bible college. When he graduated from college, he married and spent one year on the mission field in Costa Rica. When he and his wife returned from the mission field, he took a job with us. He is now a key leader in our ministry.

After David came to work for us, he and I had some serious struggles learning how to function together properly in all the different roles—parent and child, boss and employee, as well as Dave and I fulfilling the roles of spiritual leaders in his life.

David is still growing spiritually, but in God's plan. The very things that I struggled with so much in his personality as a child have become the biggest blessing to us in his role in our ministry.

We need people with management gifts whom we can trust, and David is one of those people.

God has also brought healing in my relationship with my oldest daughter.

Learning to Accept Laura

When Laura was growing up, she often forgot about things that she was supposed to do and continually lost her belongings. If she remembered to do her homework at night, she might lose it before she got to school in the morning. Or if she took it to class and turned it in, she forgot to put her name on it and received no credit for having done the work. As a result, she received only poor to mediocre grades in school.

When Laura came in the door at night from school, she left a trail of personal belongings everywhere she went. Her coat was dropped in a chair, her keys thrown on the table, her purse tossed on the couch, and her book bag plopped on the floor in the kitchen. She would go to her room, which was in shambles, and flop down in the middle of the bed and start talking on the phone.

I was born with organizational gifts and have always been a naturally disciplined person. I expected my daughter to be the same. I talked and talked, trying to get Laura to understand. And when talking didn't work, I screamed and yelled.

After Laura graduated from high school, she came to work for Joyce Meyer Ministries. At that time, our offices were located in the lower level of our home. Although we discussed with Laura the necessity of developing the employee/employer relationship, it quickly became apparent that her employment was going to present the opportunity for strife.

She was very young and had her own ideas about life and the way things should be done. She was also experiencing a mild case of rebellion. It was nothing serious, but she did not want anyone, especially Mom and Dad, telling her what to do.

Some mornings I would discover her still in the bathroom combing her hair when she should have been downstairs working. Of course, I felt I needed to tell her she had to get to work on time. The fact that the office was in our home and that she was our daughter did not matter.

Dave and I tried to explain the principles of excellence to her. We reminded her that we had other employees to consider. She nodded in agreement. Outwardly, her response was, "OK, I'll do what you say." But in her heart she felt we were wrong, and I sensed an "angry undercurrent" in her.

There were times when she wanted to get off work early to go somewhere with her boyfriend, and we had to say no. There were times when we felt she was spending too much time talking to him on the phone during working hours. I grew more and more uncomfortable, and I became concerned that our relationship would be totally ruined if something was not done. I had tried to confront the problem, but it only seemed to make it worse. What should we do? Would we actually fire our own daughter?

God had instructed Dave and me that if we would keep strife out of our marriage and ministry, He would bless us. We had been tested and tried in this area. We knew that the enemy was trying us in our relationship with our grown daughter. It was as if he was saying, "We'll see how serious you are about keeping strife out."

Dave and I talked and prayed about what to do. We both felt that it would be better for our overall relationship with her if

Laura worked somewhere else. We went to her and openly shared our feelings with her, and she agreed.

Not long after she stopped working at our ministry, Laura announced her plans to get married. She and I had more conflict around our financial obligations for the wedding, and our relationship during the months before her wedding, and even on her wedding day, was rather cool. Even though she lived just fifteen minutes from our home, we rarely saw her or heard from her during the first six months she lived away from home.

One night as I lay crying in my bed, I turned to Dave and said, "Laura doesn't love me anymore." That was a very hurtful feeling for me, as it would be for any mother. When a child rejects his or her parents, the parents are tempted to feel like total failures in the department of parenting.

Dave tried to tell me that Laura would change her mind if I would give her some time. "She just needs some time on her own," he said. "She will find out that life is a little different from how she thinks it's going to be. She will discover that Mom and Dad were not so bad after all."

When a child rejects his or her parents, the parents are tempted to feel like total failures in the department of parenting.

Dave was right. After a while, Laura came to see us more often. We were very careful not to interfere in her business because we realized that she was very sensitive about us telling her what to do. We didn't even make suggestions to her. She had stopped going to church, and we were concerned, but we knew it was important that we not hassle her about it. As a parent, it is very difficult to watch your children struggle in this area, knowing that if you try to force spiritual growth on your children, you will only make matters worse.

We needed to love our daughter right where she was and let God do what needed to be done. We prayed for her, loved her, and waited. As we continued to love Laura and accept her just as she was, she began to resist us less. We were even able to talk with her about her need to get back to regular church attendance and stop drifting away from God. She agreed, but she was not ready to work it out in her life.

I am not saying we did this without emotional suffering. It was hard for us to see Laura stay away from church when we were in full-time ministry. God is number one in our lives, and we wanted her to make Him number one in her life. She never stopped believing, but we knew she was heading for trouble if she did not make a decision. As a Christian, you either go forward or you begin to backslide. You cannot be stagnant.

Laura's first job after leaving our ministry was at a law firm. She became unhappy after a period of time and took another job at a state school for the blind. She had always enjoyed helping people that were hurting, and she felt she would be happier there. It did help for a time, because it was new, but after a while her dissatisfaction returned.

When Laura stopped working for us, we had told her that the door would always be open for her to return to work for us, but that she would need to make a spiritual commitment to God.

The time finally came when she did want to come back to work for us. She knew how she would have to live her life in order to work for the ministry, and she believed coming back to work for us would help her follow through. We had some long talks, and we all agreed to give it another try.

Laura has now worked for us for many years. She is a vital part of what we are doing. She had a job in the office for quite some time, and then the opportunity came for her husband to work for us as our soundman on the road. He held that position for quite a while before he was promoted to road manager. He is now our conference director. Both Laura and her husband have done an excellent job. We get along very well, and everyone is happy.

This began as one of those situations where being too close caused trouble. But we all matured and became wise enough to handle things. We were able to come back into good balance.

Set Your Child Free

For years I made myself—and my children—miserable in my efforts to change them. God has done with ease—and in a short period of time—what I tried to do for years in my children.

By God's grace I didn't break David's or Laura's spirits. When a child is doing his or her best, and yet their parent is continually dissatisfied, it frustrates the child and over time can break the child's spirit. Children whose spirits have been broken no longer want to try. They may give up and become rebellious as a means of defense against constant criticism. Parents need to follow Paul's advice: "Fathers,

If you love your children, set them free by accepting them as they are. If your love is true, they will come back to you.

do not irritate and provoke your children to anger [do not exasperate them to resentment], but rear them [tenderly] in the training and discipline and the counsel and admonition of the Lord" (Eph. 6:4).

Love and acceptance are the greatest gifts parents can give their children. Acceptance liberates our children to become and be who God designed them to be. Love does not try to manipulate for personal gain. It helps them overcome their weaknesses and eventually transforms them into the lovely creatures God had in mind initially. If you love your children, set them free by accepting them as they are. If your love is true, they will come back to you.

Chapter 10
Summary and Reflection

The blending of temperaments, tastes, and opinions within families can be a breeding ground for strife, particularly when parents try to change a child. The message to the child is, "You are not acceptable for who you are," and it stirs up anger and rebellion in the child. That is why God's Word says, "Fathers, do not irritate and provoke your children to anger [do not exasperate them to resentment], but rear them [tenderly] in the training and discipline and the counsel and admonition of the Lord" (Eph. 6:4).

1. Describe the different types of personalities within your family. Are some family members passive? Are certain family members strong-willed? What personality clashes cause conflict in your family?

   _____

   _____

2. What actions, attitudes, or personality do you hold that tend to fuel family strife?

   _____

   _____

3. What traits or weaknesses in family members do you find particularly annoying or difficult to deal with and accept?

   _____

   _____

4. How can you give those family members the freedom to grow without making them feel rejected? What do they need to hear you say in order to be set free?

_____

_____

5. Do you fall into regular ruts with certain family members, arguing, scolding, criticizing, or complaining about the same unresolved conflicts without experiencing any improvement? Explain.

_____

_____

6. How can you submit those ruts to God and find more peaceful ways of dealing with those conflicts?

_____

_____

_____

_____

_____

Dear heavenly Father, I give You my family members, and I ask for Your peace in all of our interactions and conflicts. I thank You for creating each one of us with our weaknesses, annoying habits, and different personality traits. Give us the grace to always see You in each other, to always accept and love each other, and to always love and accept ourselves. In Jesus's name, amen.

Part III

Unleashing God's Power and Blessings

eleven

Live in Harmony and Unity With Other Believers

T HE CHURCH IN ACTS HAD GREAT SPIRITUAL POWER. Why? "And day after day they regularly assembled in the temple with united purpose" (Acts 2:46). These believers had the same vision, the same goal, and they were all pressing toward the same mark. "And when they heard it, lifted their voices together with one united mind to God" (Acts 4:24). They prayed in agreement (Acts 4:24), lived in harmony (Acts 2:44), cared for one another (Acts 2:46), met each other's needs (Acts 4:34), and lived a life of faith (Acts 4:31). The early church as described in Acts lived in unity— and as a result, they operated in great power.

But when the church began to split into various factions with different opinions, the power of the church lessened.

People who were unable to stay in agreement due to pride and other related problems caused the church to divide into many different groups.

However, the apostle Paul told the church of Corinth that they had to get along with one another if they wanted to receive God's promised blessings. He wrote in 1 Corinthians 1:9–11, "God is faithful (reliable, trustworthy, and therefore ever true to His promise, and He can be depended on); by Him you were called into companionship and participation with His Son, Jesus Christ our Lord. But I urge and entreat you, brethren, by the name of our Lord Jesus Christ, that all of you be in perfect harmony and full agreement in what you say, and that there be no dissensions or factions or divisions among you, but that you be perfectly united in your common understanding and in your opinions and judgments. For it has been made clear to me, my brethren, by those of Chloe's household, that there are contentions [strife] and wrangling and factions among you."

The believers in the church of Corinth were people just like us, people in relationship with one another, arguing over trivial things that they should have left alone. We see that in 1 Corinthians 1:12: "What I mean is this, that each one of you [either] says, I belong to Paul, or I belong to Apollos, or I belong to Cephas (Peter), or I belong to Christ."

It sounds to me as though only the names have changed in today's arguments. Today we hear, "I'm Catholic," "I'm Lutheran," "I'm Baptist," or "I'm Pentecostal or Charismatic."

Read on to verse 13: "Is Christ (the Messiah) divided into parts? Was Paul crucified on behalf of you? Or were you baptized into the name of Paul?"

Paul was telling the Corinthians to keep their minds on Christ—not each other. If we are to live in peace with one another—and unleash God's power and blessing in our lives—we must do the same. Sometimes we get so worried and upset about what other believers are doing that we forget all about Jesus and that He has called us to live in unity with each other.

Seek to Live in Harmony and Peace

The Word of God instructs, encourages, and urges believers to live in harmony with each other. Why? Because God wants us to have blessed, powerful lives, and He knows such a life is not possible unless we live in peace.

Peace binds us to the precious Holy Spirit. God's Spirit is a spirit of peace. Jesus is the Prince of Peace. When He was ready to ascend to heaven, He told His disciples, "Peace I leave with you; My [own] peace I now give and bequeath to you. Not as the world gives do I give to you. Do not let your hearts be troubled, neither let them be afraid. [Stop allowing yourselves to be agitated and disturbed; and do not permit yourselves to be fearful and intimidated and cowardly and unsettled.]" (John 14:27).

After His resurrection Jesus appeared to His disciples. The twentieth chapter of John tells us about His appearances to His people: "Jesus came and stood among them and said, Peace to you!...Then Jesus said to them again, Peace to you!" (John 20:19, 21). Even though His disciples were behind closed doors, Jesus stood among them and said, "Peace to you!" (v. 26). I think it is apparent that Jesus was saying, "Stay in peace!"

Jesus gave us His peace for our protection. The Word says we are to "hold [our] peace" and let "peace…act as umpire" in every situation (Exod. 14:14; Col. 3:15). We should "crave peace and pursue (go after) it" and be "makers and maintainers of peace" (Ps. 34:14; Matt. 5:9).

Jesus gave us peace, but it will certainly slip away from us if we are not determined to hang on to it. God's Word tells us that if we want to live in harmony with each other, we must pursue peace and go after it. Peter wrote in his epistle: "Finally, all [of you] should be of one and the same mind [united in spirit], sympathizing [with one another], loving [each other] as brethren [of one household], compassionate and courteous (tenderhearted and humble). Never return evil for evil or insult for insult (scolding, tongue-lashing, berating), but on the contrary blessing [praying for their welfare, happiness, and protection, and truly pitying and loving them]. For know that to this you have been called, that you may yourselves inherit a blessing [from God— that you may obtain a blessing as heirs, bringing welfare and happiness and protection].

"For let him who wants to enjoy life and see good days [good—whether apparent or not] keep his tongue free from evil and his lips from guile (treachery, deceit). Let him turn away from wickedness and shun it, and let him do right. Let him search for peace (harmony; undisturbedness from fears, agitating passions, and moral conflicts) and seek it eagerly. [Do not merely desire peaceful relations with God, with your fellowmen, and with your-self, but pursue, go after them!]" (1 Pet. 3:8–11).

It's not enough to simply desire peace. We must actually live in peace in all of our relationships: our relationship with God, our relationship with others, and even our relationship with ourselves.

Paul must have understood how elusive peace can be unless we diligently seek it, because in several of his letters he urges believers to live in harmony. For example, he wrote to the Philippians: "Fill up and complete my joy by living in harmony and being of the same mind and one in purpose, having the same love, being in full accord and of one harmonious mind and intention. Do nothing from factional motives [through contentiousness, strife, selfishness, or for unworthy ends] or prompted by conceit and empty arrogance. Instead, in the true spirit of humility (lowliness of mind) let each regard the others as better than and superior to himself [thinking more highly of one another than you do of yourselves]" (Phil. 2:2–3).

> *To live in harmony we must make allowances for each other and overlook each other's mistakes and faults.*

Then, in 2 Corinthians 13:11 he said, "Finally, brethren, farewell (rejoice)! Be strengthened (perfected, completed, made what you ought to be); be encouraged and consoled and comforted; be of the same [agreeable] mind one with another; live in peace, and [then] the God of love [Who is the Source of affection, goodwill, love, and benevolence toward men] and the Author and Promoter of peace will be with you."

Paul also told the Ephesians, "Living as becomes you with complete lowliness of mind (humility) and meekness (unselfishness, gentleness, mildness), with patience, bearing with one another and making allowances because you love one another. Be eager and strive earnestly to guard and keep the harmony and oneness of [and produced by] the Spirit in the binding power of peace" (Eph. 4:2–3).

To live in harmony we must make allowances for each other and overlook each other's mistakes and faults. We must be humble, loving, compassionate, and courteous. We must be willing to forgive quickly and frequently. We must not be easily offended and must bless others rather than curse them. We must be generous in mercy, and we must be long-suffering (patient).

Harmony's "Sweet Sound"

God gave me a great illustration of what it means to live in harmony with each other while I was ministering in a church. I asked the entire worship team to return to the platform, and then I requested them to sing and play a song of their choice. I knew, of course, that they would all choose a different song because I had given no instructions on what song to sing or play. As they sang and played, the sound was horrible! There was no harmony. Then I asked them to play "Jesus Loves Me." It sounded sweet, soothing, and wonderfully comforting. Disharmony is noise in God's ears, but when we live in harmony, we produce a sweet sound.

Not only that, but when we live in peace with each other, we are actually doing spiritual warfare.

Chapter 11
Summary and Reflection

Without unity and harmony, true spiritual power cannot be released.

1. The New Testament church of the Book of Acts is a picture of unity and harmony. Acts 2:46 says, "And day after day they regularly assembled in the temple with united purpose." Describe in greater detail the characteristics of the first Christian church using the following scriptures.

   Acts 2:44

   _____

   _____

   Acts 2:46

   _____

   _____

   Acts 4:31

   _____

   _____

   Acts 4:34

   _____

   _____

2. The Word of God says, "Behold, how good and how pleasant it is for brethren to dwell together in unity! It is like the precious ointment poured on the head, that ran down the beard, even the beard of Aaron [the first high priest], that came down

upon the collar and skirts of his garments [consecrating the whole body]. It is like the dew of [lofty] Mount Hermon and the dew that comes on the hills of Zion; for there the Lord has commanded the blessing, even life forevermore [upon the high and the lowly]" (Ps. 133:1–3).

_____

_____

_____

3. Think back to a time when you were involved in a church situation that involved strife. Describe how strife got in and what happened as a result.

_____

_____

_____

4. Now think back to a time when you have personally experienced the kind of unity spoken about in Psalm 133. Write about what happened and how it made you feel.

_____

_____

_____

5. We are to pursue peace in our relationships with other believers. Do you have a present relationship in which you should attempt to pursue peace? Explain.

_____

_____

_____

6. Philippians 2:3 says, "Do nothing from factional motives [through contentiousness, strife, selfishness, or for unworthy ends] or prompted by conceit and empty arrogance. Instead,

in the true spirit of humility (lowliness of mind) let each regard the others as better than and superior to himself [thinking more highly of one another than you do of yourselves]."
Using this scripture, how might you pursue peace with that individual or group?

_____

_____

_____

Dear Lord, by the power of Your wonderful Holy Spirit, reveal to me any attitudes that have created or fueled strife among my fellow believers. I humbly repent for not being a peacemaker. Show me how I can restore peace in relationships broken or damaged through offenses and misunderstandings. I make a new commitment to become a peacemaker whenever possible with Your help. Amen.

twelve

Revise Your Strategy for Spiritual Warfare

∞

WHEN I FIRST BECAME A CHARISMATIC Christian, I listened to a lot of teaching on spiritual warfare. I had spent all of my life unsuccessfully trying to fight my own battles, and I wanted my struggles to be over. After all, I had located the culprit behind my problems—taking authority over the devil would put an end to the misery. I wanted to learn all I could to defeat him, because it was obvious he was giving me a lot of trouble, and I wanted the upper hand for a change.

So I set out to apply all the methods I had learned and was busy rebuking, resisting, casting out and off, binding and loosing, fasting and praying, and anything else that anyone told me to do. However, I could not gain victory. I had the methods, but God's power was not flowing through them. In fact, the results were minimal, and I was worn out, almost to the point of "spiritual burnout," which is what happens when we continue to do things that do not produce positive results.

Then the Lord graciously shared some truths that have become a blessing in my life. He showed me that spiritual warfare "methods" are good, but they are only carriers, or containers, for His real power. He then opened up a whole new way for me to look at spiritual warfare by challenging me to observe how Jesus dealt with the devil and how He taught us to live.

As I did so, I realized that the methods He teaches us to use to be victorious are usually the opposite of what seems to make sense in our heads. For example, He tells us to give away what we have, and we will end up with more than we started with. (See Matthew 19:21.) He says that the first shall be last, and the last shall be first. (See Matthew 19:30.) He teaches, "The way up is down; humble yourself, and I will lift you up." (See Matthew 18:4; 23:12; James 4:6; 1 Peter 5:6.)

His followers wanted Him to set up an earthly kingdom and behave as an earthly king. They wanted Him to move against the enemy in the same way that they made war. But He taught them a different way to fight their battles: "But I tell you, Love your enemies and pray for those who persecute *[hurt and abuse]* you" (Matt. 5:44).

He also said in Luke 6:27–28, "But I say to you who are listening now to Me: [in order to heed, make it a practice to] love your enemies, treat well (do good to, act nobly toward) those who detest you and pursue you with hatred, invoke blessings upon and pray for the happiness of those who curse you, implore God's blessing (favor) upon those who abuse you [who revile, reproach, disparage, and high-handedly misuse you]."

This was a brand-new way of thinking! Jesus had come to open up a "new and living way" (Heb. 10:20), one that would minister life instead of death. He conquered with meekness and gentleness. He ruled with kindness and love. He humbled Himself and was placed far above all other authority. I realized that if I wanted to experience God's power, as Jesus did, I needed to expand my definition of spiritual warfare to include obedience, peace, and love, because He stressed the importance of each of these.

> *The methods He teaches us to use to be victorious are usually the opposite of what seems to make sense in our heads.*
>
>

The Warfare of Obedience

Up until this time I had been focusing on the last part of James 4:7, which says, "Resist the devil...and he will flee." I had been busy resisting Satan, but he was not fleeing. Then the Holy Spirit opened my eyes to see the whole scripture: "So be subject to God. Resist the devil [stand firm against him], and he will flee from you." I realized that I had not been as concerned about submitting to God as I had been about resisting the devil. It was a relief to find that my obedience would unleash God's power in my life.

As we walk in obedience to God, angels assist us in our warfare. The psalmist wrote, "For He will give His angels [especial] charge over you to accompany and defend and preserve you in all your ways [of obedience and service]" (Ps. 91:11).

Angel assistance will surely make the task much easier. Angels do not just work on our behalf because we are alive, nor do they work on our behalf just because we believe Jesus is our Savior. They listen to the Word of God. As we speak God's Word and walk in obedience and service to God and others, the angels move on our behalf and protect us from principalities and powers. This does not mean that we will never experience trouble or never make a mistake; it simply means we must be serious about a lifestyle of obedience if we want God's power and blessing in our lives.

We must also wear the shoes of peace.

The Warfare of Peace

When trouble comes, our first temptation is to get upset, speak out of our emotions, and start trying first one thing and then another in the hopes of finding something that will work and turn the situation around. All of these are unacceptable behaviors for the believer who is walking in faith. None of them will bring victory. Jesus gave us peace. It is our inheritance. The devil regularly attempts to steal it, but peace is ours, and we must hold on to it. (See Exodus 14:14).

The devil cannot handle believers who know how to "hold their peace."

As believers, we are seated "in the heavenly places in Christ Jesus" (Eph. 2:6, NKJV). The word *seated* refers to rest, and the words *rest* and *peace* are equivalent to one another. The Book of Hebrews teaches us to enter the rest of God and cease from the weariness and pain of human labor. (See Hebrews 4:3, 10–11.) This peace is available to us—and has been since Jesus came, died for us, was resurrected from the dead, and ascended on high.

Peace is available, but we are encouraged to "enter" it. We enter the peace of God by believing His Word and by trusting in Him instead of in ourselves or someone else. We actually do spiritual warfare while we rest. Paul told the Philippians, "And do not [for a moment] be frightened or intimidated in anything by your opponents and adversaries, for such [constancy and fearlessness] will be a clear sign (proof and seal) to them of [their impending] destruction, but [a sure token and evidence] of your deliverance and salvation, and that from God" (Phil. 1:28).

The word *constancy* here refers to being the same—stable and consistent. Our constancy is a sign to the enemy of his impending destruction. Our rest in peace and joy during the devil's attack literally defeats him. He cannot handle believers who know how to "hold their peace." Our consistency is also an outward sign that we are trusting God, and our trust moves Him to deliver us.

We benefit when we defeat the devil, but Jesus also benefits. It gives Him glory when we operate according to His Word. He is able to bless us with our inheritance in Him. Talking about the promises of God is encouraging, but possessing them is much better. We read in Psalm 94:12–13, "Blessed (happy, fortunate, to be envied) is the man whom You discipline and instruct, O Lord, and teach out of Your law, that You may give him power to keep himself calm in the days of adversity, until the [inevitable] pit of corruption is dug for the wicked."

God's plan is to work in our lives to bring us to the place where we can keep ourselves at rest during times of adversity. The prophet Isaiah wrote, "Fear not [there is nothing to fear], for I am with you; do not look around you in terror and be dismayed, for

I am your God. I will strengthen and harden you to difficulties, yes, I will help you; yes, I will hold you up and retain you with My [victorious] right hand of rightness and justice.

"Behold, all they who are enraged and inflamed against you shall be put to shame and confounded; they who strive against you shall be as nothing and shall perish. You shall seek those who contend with you but shall not find them; they who war against you shall be as nothing, as nothing at all.

"For I the Lord your God hold your right hand; I am the Lord, Who says to you, Fear not; I will help you! Fear not, you worm Jacob, you men of Israel! I will help you, says the Lord; your Redeemer is the Holy One of Israel. Behold, I will make you to be a new, sharp, threshing instrument which has teeth; you shall thresh the mountains and beat them small, and shall make the hills like chaff.

"You shall winnow them, and the wind shall carry them away, and the tempest or whirlwind shall scatter them. And you shall rejoice in the Lord, you shall glory in the Holy One of Israel" (Isa. 41:10–16).

Here is my paraphrase of these verses: "Don't be afraid of anything. Do not allow anything to get you upset. Don't start looking all around you at the circumstances; don't start worrying. Remain peaceful; I am your God. I will help you; I will hold you up. [When we feel like we are going to cave in, we have His promise to hold us up!]

"All those in strife against you, those who come at you with a spirit of contention and war, shall end up as nothing. So hold your peace. As you hold your peace, I can work because it shows that you are trusting Me.

"I am doing a new thing in you during these trying times. I am turning you into a new, sharp, threshing machine that will mow down the enemy. Your reward will be glory and joy."

The next time something or someone threatens to steal your peace, don't give in. Instead, release God's power by holding on to your inheritance and trusting that He will take care of the situation for you.

Peace Unleashes Great Spiritual Power

If you are struggling to see peace as spiritual warfare, I understand. Our minds tell us to fight the devil with fury—not peace. How can peace win a war?

Think about a natural war for a minute. What finally puts an end to it? One or both parties decide not to fight anymore. Even if only one party decides not to fight, the other one will eventually have to quit because it no longer has anyone with whom to fight.

My husband used to make me mad because he would not fight with me. I was upset and angry, and I wanted him to say just one thing so I could rail on and on. But when Dave saw that I was just looking for an argument, he would be quiet and tell me, "I am not going to fight with you." Sometimes he would even get in the car and leave for a while, infuriating me even more, but I could not fight with someone who would not fight back.

If we meet our battles with peace and respond to the upsets in life with peace, we will experience victory. This is what Moses told the Israelites when they found the Red Sea facing them and the Egyptian army chasing them. They became frightened, and he told them, "Fear not; stand still (firm, confident, undismayed) and see the salvation of the Lord which He will work for you today. For the Egyptians you have seen today you shall never see again. The Lord will fight for you, and you shall hold your peace and remain at rest" (Exod. 14:13–14).

Notice that Moses told the Israelites to "hold their peace and remain at rest." Why? They were in warfare, and it was necessary for them to respond in peace in order to win the battle. God would fight for them if they would show their confidence in Him by being peaceful.

If you hold on to your peace, He will do the same for you.

God has given you peace. You can keep it, use it, lose it, or give it away. After all, He gave Adam dominion, and Adam gave it to Satan, who is referred to as the god of this world. The Lord God did not create Satan to be the god of this world, so how did he obtain that title? Adam gave up what God had given him.

Don't make the same mistake with those things that have been given to you through Jesus Christ. Always remember to wear your shoes of peace when you go into battle. (See Ephesians 6.) They will lead you into the warfare of love, which is also spiritual warfare.

The Warfare of Love

If we love aggressively, evil will not overtake us. Instead, we will conquer evil. "Do not let yourself be overcome by evil, but overcome (master) evil with good" (Rom. 12:21).

If love responds when strife knocks on the door, strife won't gain entrance. Instead, good will overcome evil. Light will overcome darkness. Death will be completely vanquished and swallowed up in life.

Peter admonishes us: "Above all things have intense and unfailing love for one another, for love covers a multitude of sins [forgives and disregards the offenses of others]" (1 Pet. 4:8).

We can rebuke the devil—literally scream at him until we have no voice left—but he will not flee from the person who cares nothing for obedience and the love walk. The devil brings offense, disharmony, and strife between people, but the antidote for the whole poisonous problem is love.

The devil cannot handle a lover! Jesus was always loving people and being good to them. Satan could not control Him because He walked in obedience and love. So, if you are battling the devil, you might do well to concentrate more on walking in love. I have found that at times I was concentrating so much on defeating the enemy that I had no time to be good to anyone. My war with the enemy was making me sour instead of sweet.

Satan knows that Christians who "talk the talk" but do not "walk the walk" are powerless against him. His End-Time warfare strategy is to build a stronghold of cold love. In this way he can keep the church of Jesus Christ powerless, because faith works in partnership with love.

Faith is activated, energized, and expressed through love, as we see in Galatians 5:6: "For [if we are] in Christ Jesus, neither circumcision nor uncircumcision counts for anything, but only faith activated and energized and expressed and working through love." Many people consider themselves to be great people of faith, but if you watch the fruit of their lives, you will see there is very little genuine love displayed. They may appear to be powerful, but true spiritual power is found in the facets and fruits of love, because love kills strife before it can even take root.

The Strife-Killing
Facets of Love

First Corinthians 13 tells us what love looks like: "Love endures long and is patient and kind; love never is envious nor boils over with jealousy, is not boastful or vainglorious, does not display itself haughtily. It is not conceited (arrogant and inflated with pride); it is not rude (unmannerly) and does not act unbecomingly. Love (God's love in us) does not insist on its own rights or its own way, for it is not self-seeking; it is not touchy or fretful or resentful; it takes no account of the evil done to it [it pays no attention to a suffered wrong]. It does not rejoice at injustice and unrighteousness, but rejoices when right and truth prevail.

"Love bears up under anything and everything that comes, is ever ready to believe the best of every person, its hopes are fadeless under all circumstances, and it endures everything [without weakening]. Love never fails [never fades out or becomes obsolete or comes to an end]" (vv. 4–8).

Love is like a sparkling diamond; it has many facets, including:

- Patience
- Kindness
- Generosity
- Humility
- Courtesy
- Unselfishness
- Good temper
- Guilelessness
- Sincerity

Let's examine each of these facets and think about how they can keep strife out.

Patience

"Love endures long and is patient" (1 Cor. 13:4). When people display impatience with each other or with themselves, they allow strife to come into their relationship. When we love aggressively, we are patient with each other and are able to live together in peace.

Kindness

"Love...is kind" (1 Cor. 13:4, NKJV). Strife always lurks around looking for a crack to crawl through. When we are harsh with someone, particularly someone who is distraught, we stir up anger. However, kindness acts as a healing salve. Kindness will keep strife out. "And a servant of the Lord must not quarrel but be gentle to all" (2 Tim. 2:24, NKJV).

Generosity

"Love never is envious nor boils over with jealousy" (1 Cor. 13:4). Envy and jealousy are open doors for strife. When you are tempted with jealousy, respond with generosity, and the evil will be swallowed up by the good.

At times the spirit of jealousy has attacked me relentlessly concerning someone else's ministry. I don't desire to be jealous; I hate the feeling of jealousy and envy. I have discovered that the way to combat jealousy is through generosity. Instead of playing into the devil's hands and resenting a person because of what he or she has, I frequently give to that individual so that his or her ministry can grow even more. I may not always "feel" like being generous, but I have found that generosity works to keep jealousy out.

Humility

Love "is not boastful or vainglorious, does not display itself haughtily. It is not conceited (arrogant and inflated with pride)" (1 Cor. 13:4–5). If you lack humility—if you think you are more important than other people—your life will be full of conflict and strife. Humility is a prerequisite if you want to live in peace and harmony with others. Pride goes before destruction (Prov. 16:18), but if you humble yourself, God Himself will exalt you. Many relationships have been destroyed by a spirit of strife just because neither party displayed humility and a willingness to wait for God to do the exalting.

Courtesy

Love "is not rude (unmannerly) and does not act unbecomingly" (1 Cor. 13:5). It is amazing how the words *please* or *thank you* can soften a command. Those who have authority and are in a position to tell others what to do could avoid a lot of rebellion by using better manners.

I am anointed for leadership and have always seen the ability to lead inherent in my temperament. I am direct and straightforward. As a "meat and potatoes" person, I eliminate the frills and just get to the main issue. This is a good quality, but it can also be abrasive if it is not tempered with courtesy. I may have been "born a boss," but I don't need to be bossy—there is a big difference.

For relationships to remain harmonious, we need to treat each other with courtesy. We need to engage in the pleasantries of life. They may not be vital, but it's wise to use them because they can prevent tension and rebellion. I am the boss, and I can simply tell people what to do. If they want to work for me, they have to do as I ask. But if I take the extra time to be courteous, they will *want* to work for our ministry for a long time.

Courtesy is also vital in our relationships with our family and friends. I have found that we have a tendency to take liberties with those closest to us that we wouldn't consider taking with a total stranger. I recall the Holy Spirit correcting me years ago for the rude way I was speaking to my husband. He said, "Joyce, if you would be as courteous to Dave as you are to your pastor, your marriage would be a lot better." A lot of strife can be avoided by simple courtesy. I encourage you to go the extra mile to be courteous with your family and closest friends.

Unselfishness

"Love (God's love in us) does not insist on its own rights or its own way, for it is not self-seeking" (1 Cor. 13:5). The New King James translation says that love "does not seek its own."

Jesus is love, and if we intend to follow His lifestyle, it will require the development of an unselfish nature. He told His disciples (and us), "If anyone intends to come after Me, let him deny himself [forget, ignore, disown, and lose sight of himself and his own interests]" (Mark 8:34). Since Christ is in us, the seed for that nature is already in us, but we must choose to develop it. God has planted His seed in us, but we must water and care for it properly so it grows to the fruit-bearing stage. The giving up of oneself is no easy task. The flesh dies hard and fights relentlessly.

Strife was a constant visitor in our home when I lived in selfishness. Selfishness is the breeding ground for strife. Over the years, as God has dealt with me, I have become less selfish, and my life and relationships have become much more harmonious. Strife has lost its nesting place.

Self-control

Love "is not touchy or fretful or resentful" (1 Cor. 13:5). It "is not provoked, thinks no evil" (NKJV). It is slow to anger (James 1:19). The antidote for a quick temper is self-control, which is a fruit of the Spirit. (See Galatians 5:22–23.)

> *Since Christ is in us, the seed for an unselfish nature is already in us, but we must choose to develop it.*

If you struggle with a quick temper, ask God to reveal the root of the problem. Perhaps you suffered abuse in the past, and you have some repressed anger that you need to deal with. Or maybe you are proud and need humility. Pride is often the root of a quick temper.

My daughters had problems with anger and finally saw that it was rooted in perfectionism. I have learned that using self-control to control the emotion of anger is much easier than trying to deal with all the repercussions once I lose my temper. I hate strife and its effects on people. A good temper will slam the door in strife's face.

Guilelessness

Love "thinks no evil" (1 Cor. 13:5, NKJV). We need to guard our thoughts because they have the power to produce good or evil in our lives. Each of us has both the mind of the flesh and the mind of the spirit, as Romans 8:6 tells us, but we are to choose the mind of the Spirit, which will produce life and peace.

Love is good and expects the best of every person. How is it possible to expect the best from people who have disappointed us time after time? Love forgets the past and deals with each issue in a fresh way. Oh, how glorious it would be to be totally guileless. Just imagine the inner peace in the person who never has an evil thought. You may think, "This sounds great in theory, but is it really possible?" I do not know if I will ever attain this perfection, but I am determined to press on toward the goal. Lovely thinking defeats strife!

Sincerity

"[Let your] love be sincere (a real thing); hate what is evil [loathe all ungodliness, turn in horror from wickedness], but hold fast to that which is good" (Rom. 12:9). Love is sincere. It's not just a lot of talk or theory, but it is seen in action. Love meets needs. Love is genuine. It really wants to help others.

Love Unleashes Great Spiritual Power

Before Paul talks about the facets and fruit of love, he says, "If I [can] speak in the tongues of men and [even] of angels, but have not love (that reasoning, intentional, spiritual devotion such as is inspired by God's love for and in us), I am only a noisy gong or a clanging cymbal.

"And if I have prophetic powers (the gift of interpreting the divine will and purpose), and understand all the secret truths and mysteries and possess all knowledge, and if I have [sufficient] faith so that I can remove mountains, but have not love (God's love in me) I am nothing (a useless nobody).

171

"Even if I dole out all that I have [to the poor in providing] food, and if I surrender my body to be burned or in order that I may glory, but have not love (God's love in me), I gain nothing" (1 Cor. 13:1–3).

According to this passage, if we don't walk in love, all our efforts to serve God and demonstrate His power will be fruitless. Love is the greatest power in the world. It makes life worth living. It sets us free from the Law. "And so faith, hope, love abide...but the greatest of these is love" (1 Cor. 13:13). Paul instructs us that love is the "more excellent way" to live (1 Cor. 12:31). He prayed that "your love may abound...may display itself" (Phil. 1:9). Without love, we "gain nothing" (1 Cor. 13:3).

If we love aggressively, we will resist strife every time. Satan knows this, so he wants to keep us from walking in love. He knows that if we develop our love walk, we will be dangerous to the kingdom of darkness. It is quite easy, because of the nature of the flesh, for us to become selfish and self-centered. But with God's help and a willing heart, we can enjoy harmonious and conflict-free relationships that manifest the true spirit of love.

Have a "Holy Determination"

Strife comes like a raging storm and leaves destruction everywhere it is permitted to go. But you can defeat it by holding fast to that which is good. Grasp the importance of peace and love. They are essential to a life of victory, power, and blessing. If you want to experience those things, let a holy determination rise up within you to walk in peace and to walk in love. Determine to hold on to your peace and to love aggressively—and then stand back and see what God does in you and through you.

Chapter 12
Summary and Reflection

Spiritual warfare to defeat the devil can be accomplished through powerful weapons that we often hear little about—such as obedience, peace, and love.

1. The Bible says, "So be subject to God. Resist the devil [stand firm against him], and he will flee from you" (James 4:7). Why do you suppose submitting to God is just as important as resisting the devil?

2. Have you ever experienced an attack from an individual to destroy your character, position, or reputation? Use Matthew 5:44 and Luke 6:27 to describe how you might respond biblically.

3. Paraphrase Isaiah 41:10–16, using your own words to describe God's promise to keep you at peace during life's storms.

4. The principles of Christianity are often paradoxical. In other words, they seem completely upside down. Using the following scriptures,

write about events from your own life that illustrate the use or lack of use of these principles.

Matthew 18:4

_____

_____

Matthew 19:21

_____

_____

Matthew 19:30

_____

_____

Matthew 23:12

_____

_____

James 4:6

_____

_____

1 Peter 5:6

_____

_____

5. Paraphrase 1 Corinthians 13:1–8.

_____

_____

_____

6. Think about a time when you were in conflict with another person. How could you have used love as a spiritual weapon to defeat the strategies of Satan in that situation?

_____

_____

_____

_____

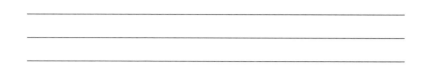

Dear Lord, give me the grace to respond to the battles in my life with obedience, peace, and love. I submit my life to You, knowing that You hold my future in Your hands. I submit my future battles to You before they even happen, and I ask You to cause me to triumph through the power of Your peace and love. Help me to walk in unselfishness, generosity, and goodwill toward others. Where my heart is small, make it large with Your love. Amen.

thirteen

Press Forward Into Change—Don't Fight It

∽∞∽

As Joyce Meyer Ministries has grown, we've had to make certain changes. Things we could do when we had only five employees just won't work now. Our ministry has expanded, and so has the amount of work required to get the job done.

Our workday used to be from 8:00 a.m. to 4:30 p.m., allowing thirty minutes for lunch. However, when we went on television with our ministry, we wanted to keep the office open as long as possible for people to place orders for tapes, and so we changed our work hours and extended the lunch hour. None of our employees complained, but I am sure that some of them liked the change while others did not.

This is only one of many changes the people who work in our ministry have gone through. It's impossible to go through life and not experience numerous changes. We all have personal preferences for things, so some changes work out better for us than others. Some changes we like and readily accept; others we dislike and sometimes resist.

Since change is unavoidable, we need to understand how it affects us so that we press forward into it rather than fight it and open the door to strife. When we embrace change rather than resist it, we are more likely to continue to live in harmony with others, thereby unleashing the flow of God's power and blessing in our lives.

Understanding How Change Affects Us

When people move, change jobs, lose relationships, or make new relationships—and thousands of other types of changes—they are under a certain amount of pressure. Change means dealing with the unknown. We like to have all our ducks in a row and to know exactly what's happening each step of the way. When something changes, things are different. This can be threatening as well as taxing. Change always requires more of our attention.

For instance, when we are developing new relationships with people, we must learn how they react in every situation. What things do they like? What do they dislike? What is acceptable to say to them? What is not? Will they get offended if we tease them?

Getting to know someone demands much more of our energy than what is required to simply be with a good friend we have known for a long time. The stress this creates can shorten our fuse in other areas.

In fact, any kind of change can add stress to our lives, which can make us irritable and tense. Some women, for example, are difficult to live with during their monthly cycle. Why? Because their bodies are changing and they feel different. If they don't get more rest and avoid potentially stressful situations, they are more vulnerable to conflict during this time. Within a few days they are able to handle wonderfully something that they could not handle at all during the time of their physical changes.

Change means dealing with the unknown.

The same is true for women who are going through the change of life. Their bodies are undergoing drastic changes, and often middle-aged women find that their bodies can no longer bounce back the way they did before. These physical changes affect some women more than others, but for many, it's a season of change that can open doors for strife in relationships.

If a woman's patience level is low and the noise level in her home is high, she may get angry. Things she was quite satisfied with before may suddenly become unacceptable. If her husband does not give her the affection she desires, she may be more easily hurt, and so withdraw and act in ways that her family is not used to. Her need for affection apart from sex may increase during this time. She wants to be held, but nothing more.

In order to avoid conflict during such a stressful change, it helps for a woman to remember that her husband cannot read her mind. She needs to remember that she is changing, but her family is just the same as always. They do not feel the way she does and should not be expected to understand her without some education.

When I went through the change of life, it helped me to say to myself, "Joyce, you are feeling these changes, but everything is going to be all right." Talk to yourself sometimes; have a heart-to-heart conversation with yourself. Do not allow change to disorient you to the point that it causes strife.

Some people have difficulty when their church or organization undergoes some kind of change. Perhaps the pastor feels that God is leading his church into a strong foreign missions outreach program. Some members of his congregation may think it's great, while others may feel that an inner-city outreach program would be better. When people fail to realize that many of their feelings are based on their own opinions and preferences, they can quickly open a door for strife by vocalizing their disagreement. It's a mistake to assume that a leader is not following God's will just because you don't agree personally with a change he or she makes. This can cause an unbelievable amount of conflict and destruction in a church.

Whenever you are facing changes of any kind, remember the devil will try to take advantage of you. He hopes to catch you off guard so you will let him in without realizing what's happening.

That's why, if your workplace, church, or some other organization you are involved with undergoes a change that you dislike, the wise thing to do is to give it some time to see how the change really affects you. Give things a chance to settle. If after the period of waiting you still feel the same way, talk to the person responsible for the change. Once you understand the situation and why the change was made, your entire outlook may change.

If you've done this and find that you still can't be happy with the change, consider leaving, but leave in peace. Do not gossip and complain to others. Do not leave assuming that everyone else is wrong. What they are doing may be right for their business, church, or organization, but not right for you. We are to give one another liberty and not be judgmental. The apostle Paul wrote, "One [man's faith permits him to] believe he may eat anything, while a weaker one [limits his] eating to vegetables. Let not him who eats look down on or despise him who abstains, and let not him who abstains criticize and pass judgment on him who eats; for God has accepted and welcomed him.

"Who are you to pass judgment on and censure another's household servant? It is before his own master that he stands or falls. And he shall stand and be upheld, for the Master (the Lord) is mighty to support him and make him stand. One man esteems one day as better than another, while another man esteems all days alike [sacred]. Let everyone be fully convinced (satisfied) in his own mind" (Rom. 14:2–5).

Another kind of change that can open the door to strife occurs during those times when God is dealing with us. When the Lord is dealing with us on the inside, He intends to bring change on the outside. These changes are designed to bring progress, and Satan will always fight progress.

Is Satan Trying to Disrupt a Change God Wants to Make *in* You?

God changes us in ever-increasing degrees of glory. His goal is to make us more like Himself: "And all of us, as with unveiled face, [because we] continued to behold [in the Word of God] as in a mirror the glory of the Lord, are constantly being transfigured into His very own image in ever increasing splendor and from one

181

degree of glory to another; [for this comes] from the Lord [Who is] the Spirit" (2 Cor. 3:18).

In order to accomplish this goal, God sometimes disciplines us for our ultimate good. However, while the discipline is taking place, it isn't much fun. Hebrews 12:11 tells us, "For the time being no discipline brings joy, but seems grievous and painful; but afterwards it yields a peaceable fruit of righteousness to those who have been trained by it [a harvest of fruit which consists in righteousness—in conformity to God's will in purpose, thought, and action, resulting in right living and right standing with God]."

God's discipline changes us and makes us more like Jesus in our thoughts, words, and actions. His plan is to bring us into a new realm of glory, which Satan doesn't want. Consequently, the devil will oppose us persistently if we are going forward. He delights in getting us distracted and preventing us from pressing in with God.

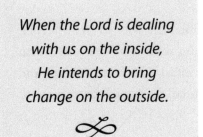

When the Lord is dealing with us on the inside, He intends to bring change on the outside.

Many times over the years I have sensed God speaking to me about changes that need to take place within my ministry in order for it to grow to the next level. However, I know that change is frequently very difficult for people. Because I love people and don't want to hurt or disappoint them, I have sometimes found it difficult to obey God in this area.

It is challenging to tell a person who is doing their best that the position they have has outgrown them and that we need to make a change. Many times it involves people who have done a great job for years; they are easy to get along with and are very committed to their job, but they have reached their ceiling. If I don't make the changes God is asking me to make, their ceiling creates one for the ministry and prevents our growth. Since ministry growth means an opportunity to reach more people for Jesus, my decision cannot be based on what would be easy for me or what would not hurt their feelings.

I have learned through experience that if I don't obey God because I don't want to hurt the person, I usually hurt them more in the long run. If God is asking me to make a change, then He also has a new thing for them to do—something that they will enjoy even more than what they are doing for us. The fear of change keeps a lot of people from making progress, and it leads to disobedience.

How are we to respond to times of discipline and change (times when God is changing us)? The following verses provide an answer: "You must submit to and endure [correction] for discipline; God is dealing with you as with sons. For what son is there whom his father does not [thus] train and correct and discipline?...So then, brace up and reinvigorate and set right your slackened and weakened and drooping hands and strengthen your feeble and palsied and tottering knees, and cut through and make firm and plain and smooth, straight paths for your feet [yes, make them safe and upright and happy paths that go in the right direction], so that the lame and halting [limbs] may not be put out of joint, but rather may be cured" (Heb. 12:7, 12–13).

A footnote to the thirteenth verse in the Worrell New Testament reads as follows: "Make straight paths for your feet; choose God's Word to be a 'lamp to your feet, and a light to your path'

(Ps. 119:105, WNT); not only for your good and the glory of God, but also on account of others, who will be helped or injured by your example."

When God disciplines us, it can be uncomfortable and painful. That's why we are told "submit to" and "endure" His discipline in our lives. We are to "choose God's Word to be a 'lamp to our feet and a light to our path.'" The instructions continue in verse 14, where it says we are to "strive to live in peace with everybody and pursue that consecration and holiness without which no one will [ever] see the Lord." We are to press forward and pursue holiness by allowing God to work in us while we strive to live in peace with everyone.

How can we accomplish this? How can we "strive to live in peace" during those stressful times in our lives when we are at war with ourselves because God is trying to bring about some change in us?

1. *Let others know that God is dealing with you.* When God is dealing with us, we don't always understand what He is doing and why. We can feel confused because we can't make sense of all the things we are feeling inside, and this can be a source of conflict with those we are close to, if we don't guard against it. For this reason Dave and I have learned to tell each other when we believe that God is dealing with us. We might say, "God is dealing with me. I don't know about what yet, but I know something is going on inside me, so if I act a little unusual or seem quieter, that's why."

   Before we started letting each other know when God was trying to change us, such times often opened doors for strife between us. If I were behaving differently, and Dave did not understand why because I had not bothered to tell him the reason, he would become quiet. Then I thought something was wrong with him and became even more aggravated because I thought I already had enough to deal with without him getting weird on me.

2. *Practice self-control.* Another thing I have learned is that I do not have the right to display every feeling I have. If God is dealing with me, I must let Him do it without becoming melodramatic and making a lot more out of the situation than it warrants.

We can learn to go through the changes God brings into our lives without taking our frustrations out on others. We can, and should, learn to bear the good fruit of the Holy Spirit during times of change.

Sometimes the change God wants to make has to do with what He wants to accomplish through us.

Is Satan Trying to Hinder a New Thing God Wants to Accomplish *Through* You?

During my years in ministry, I have found that the Holy Spirit sometimes shows me things on the horizon ahead of time so I can begin preparing myself in that area. I believe we are approaching a time in the body of Christ when we will see a great deal of physical healings. I have had confirmation about this from other people in ministry who also sense God leading in that direction. Since I could, in this instance, see what is ahead, I knew I needed to start studying, praying, and seeking God in the area of healing the sick. Preparation is vital to being used by God

I heard from God about how He wanted me to proceed, and I began. Within twenty-four hours, I got sidetracked from my study because I had to deal with three different employees who were suddenly in need of some serious correction. I do not mean to imply that any of these employees are "bad" people. My point is that the devil stirs up anything he can to get us distracted when God is trying to do something in us or through us. Satan uses strife to prevent our progress. He will try to work through whatever weaknesses a person has (and we all have some) at a time when we are about to break through into a brand-new glory in our lives.

All three employees are precious people who have hurts and wounds in their past that they are working through. We are trying to help them, and in doing so we must deal with issues from time to time. They have been wounded emotionally, and sometimes their emotions get a bit out of hand. The enemy knows he can push the right buttons and stir up their emotions. In time this weakness will be controlled by the Holy Spirit and become a strength for these people. But for now, it's an area that Satan can use if they are not aware of his cunning manipulation. Since they work for us, if he gets them stirred up, I end up having to deal with it.

We make the mistake of thinking that people are the problem, when our true enemy is the spirit of strife.

At first, I didn't realize what was happening, which is exactly what Satan wants. When he can keep the truth from us, he is in control and we do not know what is really going on behind the scenes. But when all three individuals "happened" to have a problem on the same day, it became obvious to me that "unseen" forces were at work

Then, within that same twenty-four-hour period, something came up with one of our sons that Dave and I had a difference of opinion about. All parents have to deal with these situations from time to time. I felt one way, and my husband felt another. It was not a long-term problem, but each time it came up, I had to sit on my emotions and remember that Dave is the head of our household. When he and I disagree, I can say what I think in a respectful manner, but then, I need to leave the final decision to him and remain at peace. Even though I know what I should do, doing it still requires a certain amount of my attention.

I believe Satan arranged for this particular instance to occur precisely at a time when he knew it could upset me and could initiate tension and conflict between Dave and me. The devil certainly does not want me to progress in a healing ministry. He does not want me to study and gain new revelation. He does not want me to help more people and see their suffering relieved. He fights against the church and her progress with many things, but as I've been saying throughout this book, one of his favorite weapons is dissension. We make the mistake of thinking that people are the problem, when our true enemy is the spirit of strife.

No wonder Matthew 26:41 says that we are to "watch and pray." We must watch ourselves and watch how the enemy is trying to work through other people and circumstances to prevent our progress and block the flow of God's blessing and power in our lives. We must also guard against allowing Satan to use our own problems as a way of hindering the work of the Lord in another person's life.

What was I to do in these four situations? The answer can provide some principles for how you can resist strife so that Satan doesn't hinder a new thing that God may want to do through your own life.

1. *Press forward, being sure to do what God has called you to do.* It was my responsibility to deal with the problem, but it was also important that I keep pressing forward in my study concerning healing the sick.

2. *Deal with the problem, but don't give in to the temptation to get upset and aggravated.* I needed to deal with each individual involved in a godly way, not allowing myself to get all upset and aggravated about it.

   At times I get aggravated with something that needs to be dealt with. Dave has often told me that if I would spend the time dealing with the issue that I spend being upset about it, it would be taken care of and finished. He is right, of course, but I have had to learn this.

   I now know that people who deal with a lot of other people will always have things to handle. That does not mean the people are bad; it's just the way life is. God wants us to walk in love and to support one another, edifying and strengthening each other and promoting one another's progress.

3. *Trust God to tell you what to say.* Satan wants strife, arguing, judgment, offense, and weakness. He knows that he can weaken the strength of any group by bringing division. We need to pray and trust God to lead us to say the right things to them. We don't need to spend all day and night mentally "rehearsing" what we will say to them. Satan wants to fill our mind with just such useless thoughts.

Think about it. How often have you spent hours rehearsing your words to someone you needed to confront, and yet when the time came, you did not say any of it? All that "mental time" was wasted. Far better to have spent the same time meditating on the Word or thinking about the goodness of God.

If we trust the Lord, He will lead us in what we are to say at the right time. I should give a reasonable amount of thought to what I say in order to be properly prepared, but getting out of balance allows the devil to waste my time and prevent my progress.

The next time you are going through some kind of change, remember that the devil will see this time of added stress in our life as an opportunity to stir up problems and the potential for conflict. Be on guard. Times of change are often hard, but they lead us into new realms of glory.

If God is trying to bring about some change in you, tell the people in your life who will be affected by what is going on in you, but go on about your business and let God do what He needs to do. Allow Him to do His work in you. Watch and pray, and be wise to the enemy's strategies and deceits.

Chapter 13
Summary and Reflection

When we are undergoing changes at home, at work, or at church, it can produce enormous stress, which makes us more vulnerable to strife. We need to be on guard during such times and press forward and trust God with the situation so that His power and blessing can flow unhindered into our lives.

1. Have you undergone a change in the recent past or present that has been difficult to deal with? Is your opposition to certain changes based on your own opinions or on God's Word? Explain.

   My own opinions. Very Over
   _____

   _____

2. Did you or have you given the changes enough time to see if they will work out for you?

   _____

   _____

   _____

3. Are you willing to speak with those in leadership about your feelings instead of sharing them with everyone else? How can you approach them in a way that will pursue peace?

   _____

   _____

   _____

4. If you are no longer able to be happy in the situation because of the changes that have taken place, do you love the organization and its people enough to be willing to leave rather than cause strife?

_____

_____

_____

5. Describe a time when God was trying to bring a change in you or through you and how you "suffered in silence" or took your frustrations out on others.

_____

_____

_____

6. How will you "press forward" into such changes in the future?

_____

_____

_____

_____

Lord, I surrender my life to You in all my seasons and situations of changes—past, present, and future. Keep me from allowing change to bring me into strife. Help me to draw nearer to You during times and seasons of change. Let me sense Your strength, Your power, and Your peace during such times. And Lord, when I need extra help to stay calm and peaceful, please help me to draw closer to Your heart. In Jesus's name, amen.

fourteen

Protect the Anointing

∞

SEVERAL YEARS AGO I FELT LED TO TEACH ON THE subject of peace. I spent an entire day sitting in the middle of my bed studying. I felt as if I were looking for something concerning the subject of peace, and yet I did not know what it was. I searched the Scriptures, waiting for the light of revelation to come to me, and came across this passage: "Now after this the Lord chose and appointed seventy others and sent them out ahead of Him, two by two, into every town and place where He Himself was about to come (visit). And He said to them, The harvest indeed is abundant [there is much ripe grain], but the farmhands are few. Pray therefore the Lord of the harvest to send out laborers into His harvest. Go your way; behold, I send you out like lambs into the midst of wolves.

"Carry no purse, no provisions bag, no [change of] sandals; refrain from [retarding your journey by] saluting and wishing anyone well along the way. Whatever house you enter, first say, Peace be to this household! [Freedom from all the distresses that result from sin be with this family].

"And if anyone [worthy] of peace and blessedness is there, the peace and blessedness you wish shall come upon him; but if not, it shall come back to you. And stay on in the same house, eating and drinking what they provide, for the laborer is worthy of his wages. Do not keep moving from house to house" (Luke 10:1–7).

As I read, I saw something that I had never seen previously in these verses. I felt the Lord was showing me that peace and power go together. When Jesus sent the disciples out to heal the sick and proclaim the kingdom of God, He told them to find a peaceful place to reside and stay there. He told them that they needed a "base of operations" that was peaceful. I felt the Holy Spirit saying to me, "Joyce, if you want to have a powerful ministry that will help multitudes, find peace and stay in it."

At that time I was not very peaceful. I still had a lot of inner turmoil, and I still caused a lot of upset in my relationships with others. I had not yet learned the importance of conflict-free living. The Spirit showed me that just as He told the disciples to find a peaceful place and let that be their base of operation, I was to be His house—His base of operation—and He wanted the house He was working in to be peaceful.

I wanted to minister under a strong anointing, and I had been praying about it regularly. God was answering my prayer by showing me what I needed to do to enable the anointing to flow.

Why Peace and Power
Go Together

God's anointing is always resident in the believer. The apostle John wrote in his epistle, "But you have been anointed by [you hold a sacred appointment from, you have been given an unction from] the Holy One, and you all know [the Truth] or you know all things. . . . But as for you, the anointing (the sacred appointment, the unction) which you received from Him abides [permanently] in you; [so] then you have no need that anyone should instruct you. But just as His anointing teaches you concerning everything and is true and is no falsehood, so you must abide in (live in, never depart from) Him [being rooted in Him, knit to Him], just as [His anointing] has taught you [to do]" (1 John 2:20, 27).

While believers always have the anointing, the manifestation of the anointing is vital to powerful living and powerful ministry. As we have seen, strife definitely hinders the flow of God's power: "And do not grieve the Holy Spirit of God [do not offend or vex or sadden Him], by Whom you were sealed (marked, branded as God's own, secured) for the day of redemption (of final deliverance through Christ from evil and the consequences of sin). Let all bitterness and indignation and wrath (passion, rage, bad temper) and resentment (anger, animosity) and quarreling (brawling, clamor, contention) and slander (evil-speaking, abusive or blasphemous language) be banished from you, with all malice (spite, ill will, or baseness of any kind). And become useful and helpful and kind to one another, tenderhearted (compassionate, understanding, loving-hearted), forgiving one another [readily and freely], as God in Christ forgave you" (Eph. 4:30–32).

Strife grieves the Holy Spirit and will separate us from the power and anointing of the Spirit. However, the power of peace binds us to the Holy Spirit, as we see in Ephesians 4:3: "Be eager and strive earnestly to guard and keep the harmony and oneness of [and produced by] the Spirit in the binding power of peace."

One might say that peace and power live together. They are married; they support each other.

The Power of the Anointing

The anointing of the Holy Spirit is one of the most important things in my life and ministry. It ushers me into the presence and the power of God. The anointing manifests in ability, enablement, and strength. The anointing ministers life to me. I feel alive and strong physically when the anointing is flowing, as well as mentally alert.

When we live in peace and harmony, we unleash God's anointing for more than just ministry. I believe there is an anointing for everything that we are called to do—not just for spiritual things. We can be anointed for cleaning the house, for doing laundry, for leading a home or business, or for being a student. God's presence makes everything easy and enjoyable.

People laugh when I say this, but there is an anointing that comes on me to shop. If it's there, the trip is very fruitful and enjoyable. If it's not, I cannot find anything I am looking for. I can't seem to make decisions about what to buy. Even if I find something I like, I don't seem to have any real desire to buy it. I say in times like that, "If I buy anything today, it will have to jump off the rack and just get on my body."

What other kinds of things may we expect to be anointed for? I believe a woman can go to the grocery store and be anointed by God to shop for her family's groceries if she will exercise her faith to release the anointing. If she gets upset with the grocery store because they don't have some items she wants, the anointing will stop flowing for her trip until she returns to a peaceful state and the strife disappears.

> *I believe there is an anointing to go to your place of work and to enjoy being there.*

I believe there is an anointed sleep we can enjoy when we go to bed at night. However, if a person lies in bed and thinks of some situation that is full of strife, he or she is not likely to sleep well due to fretful dreams or tossing and turning all night.

I believe there is an anointing to go to your place of work and to enjoy being there. The anointing will also help you do your job with ease. Again, if you have strife with your boss or with other employees, the anointing will be blocked. Whether the strife is open or hidden within your heart, the effect is the same.

So, keep strife out so that you can live by the anointing. God has given it to you to help you in all that you do. Things are not accomplished by might or power, but by His Spirit. (See Zechariah 4:6.) Stay peaceful and calm; be quick to forgive, slow to anger, patient, and kind. Protect the anointing in your life, and sow good seeds by helping others do the same. In so doing, you will reap a harvest in your own time of need.

Protect the Anointing

The Word of God teaches us to watch out for one another. This is part of the love walk. We read in Hebrews 12:14–15, "Strive to live in peace with everybody and pursue that consecration and holiness without which no one will [ever] see the Lord. Exercise foresight and be on the watch to look [after one another], to see that no one falls back from and fails to secure God's grace."

We can help our loved ones walk in peace by maintaining peace, especially when we know they are already under pressure. For instance, my family knows that just before one of our services, I am busy meditating on what God has given me to minister that day. I have asked them to refrain from telling me anything right before a meeting that would tend to be upsetting. They help me by trying to keep the atmosphere peaceful.

We can help each other to avoid strife by being a little more sensitive to one another's needs. For example:

- When a husband comes home from an especially trying day at the office, his wife can minister peace to him by directing the children into an activity that creates a calmer atmosphere rather than a chaotic one.

- When a wife has been cleaning and cooking all day for a special holiday family get-together the next day, her husband can minister peace to her by taking the children somewhere for the evening so that she can have a nice long block of quiet time.

- If a child has been taking final exams for a week and is already under stress, the parents might choose to withhold correction for a messy room or leaving a bike out on the driveway until the stress of the exams has ended.

After being married to Dave for more than forty years, I can tell when he is tired or not feeling good. I have learned to minister peace to him at those times instead of bringing up a problem to him right then. He is a very peaceful man and would probably handle himself quite well even if I did bring up a problem, but there is no point in adding weight to an already heavy load.

Grace is unmerited favor. We can do others a favor and help them protect the anointing by not placing undue pressure upon them during times when they are most vulnerable to strife. For me, this time is when I am getting ready to minister. For you, it may be some other time or circumstance. It's important to know when you are most likely to succumb to conflict so that you can protect the anointing and experience God's power in all of your life.

Jesus had multiple opportunities to be in strife, and yet, without hesitation, He turned every one of them down. Even as He hung on the cross He prayed, "Father, forgive them, for they know not what they do" (Luke 23:34). Judas, Herod, Pilate, and the Pharisees all presented Him with opportunities for strife. He turned every one of them into an opportunity to show forth His Father's character. Instead of strife, He responded with gentleness, courtesy, and patience.

With His help, you can do the same. You can meet the enemy head-on. Paul wrote to Timothy (and to us), "But refuse (shut your mind against, have nothing to do with) trifling (ill-informed, unedifying, stupid) controversies over ignorant questionings, for you know that they foster strife and breed quarrels. And the servant of the Lord must not be quarrelsome (fighting and contending). Instead, he must be kindly to everyone and mild-tempered [preserving the bond of peace]" (2 Tim. 2:23–24).

The anointing of God is upon you for whatever your task. Don't give it up in order to satisfy some fleshly emotion that is pushing you to act like the devil instead of God. Don't block the flow by allowing strife in your life. Be all that God has called you to be. Live at peace with yourself, with God, and with others.

> *We can do others a favor and help them protect the anointing by not placing undue pressure upon them during times when they are most vulnerable to strife.*

Chapter 14
Summary and Reflection

The anointing of the Holy Spirit is resident in you to empower, strengthen, enlighten, and equip you for ministry.

1. Strife and bitterness grieve the Holy Spirit. According to Ephesians 4:30–32, what is the scriptural antidote for strife?

   _____

   _____

2. In the same way that strife repels the Holy Spirit, the power of peace binds the Holy Spirit to us. What attitudes will help you to never grieve the Holy Spirit, according to Ephesians 4:30–32?

   _____

   _____

3. The Lord sent the disciples to go out and find a "base of operations" that was peaceful. Read Luke 10:1–7 and explain why you believe the Lord gave this command.

   _____

   _____

4. Is your "base of operations" peaceful, whether it be your home, job, church, or circle of friends? What can you do to make your environment more peaceful?

   _____

   _____

5. How can you help others protect the anointing in their lives?

_____

_____

_____

_____

_____

6. What can you do to protect the anointing in your own life?

_____

_____

_____

_____

_____

Dear Father, grant me the grace to live in and operate in an environment of peace. Show me what attitudes and habits I have that might be contributing to strife. Provide me with Your divine strategy for being a peacemaker wherever I go. In Jesus's name, amen.

fifteen

Reclaim Your Inheritance

∽

You and I are joint heirs with Jesus Christ. Jesus said in John 16:15, "Everything that the Father has is Mine. That is what I meant when I said that He [the Spirit] will take the things that are Mine and will reveal (declare, disclose, transmit) it to you."

Everything the Father has is yours through Jesus. His kingdom is one of righteousness, peace, and joy. Whatever is in right standing with Him will produce right thoughts, words, and actions, and this too is yours. Supernatural peace and joy, which are not based on positive or negative circumstances, belong to you as a believer. Look at what John 14:27 says: "Peace I leave with you; My [own] peace I now give and bequeath to you. Not as the world gives do I give to you. Do not let your hearts be troubled, neither let them be afraid.

[Stop allowing yourselves to be agitated and disturbed; and do not permit yourselves to be fearful and intimidated and cowardly and unsettled.]"

Jesus became the blood sacrifice that atoned for and completely removed your sin in order for you to live in peace.

In essence, Jesus was saying, "I am willing you My peace. I am going away, and the thing I desire to leave you is My peace." His special peace is a wonderful possession. How valuable is peace? What is it worth?

Peace was worth the shedding of His blood. The prophet Isaiah said, "But He was wounded for our transgressions, He was bruised for our guilt and iniquities; the chastisement [needful to obtain] peace and well-being for us was upon Him, and with the stripes [that wounded] Him we are healed and made whole" (Isa. 53:5).

Jesus became the blood sacrifice that atoned for and completely removed your sin in order for you to live in peace. God's will for you is that you live in peace with Him, with yourself, and with others. He wants you to have peace in the midst of your current circumstances—whether they are good or bad. He wants you to have peace in the morning, at night, and all times in between. Peace is your inheritance!

Peace and enjoyment of life go hand in hand. You can enjoy life more with an abundance of peace. Peace is glorious—and it is your inherited right. Peace is yours through the "bloodline" of Jesus.

Are you experiencing supernatural peace and joy? What is going on inside of you? Is the atmosphere peaceful? Joyful?

If not, you need to reclaim your inheritance. You need to reclaim the peace and joy that are yours. To do so, you need to do the following:

Ask God to Reveal the Root of the Problem

Satan does not want you to know what is robbing you of peace and joy. He wants you to run around in circles, so to speak, always looking for something and never discovering anything. It is important to remember that we do not war with flesh and blood. Many times our problems are not what we think, but they have their roots in subtle, hidden strife.

In this way, Satan deceives people. They spend their lives attempting to deal with the wrong issues. For instance, has it ever occurred to you that confusion is strife in your mind? People who are confused argue with themselves. Their thoughts fly back and forth in conflict with each other. A double-minded person is not at peace.

Worry is also a form of strife. Many mothers think they are not good mothers if they don't worry about their children. They are deceived. These women love the Lord, but they are not experiencing God's blessing in their lives—they are not experiencing supernatural joy. Their minds are not peaceful; they are filled with worry, anxiety, and turmoil. Worry leads to emotional upset. In John 14:27, Jesus advises, "Stop allowing yourselves to be agitated and disturbed."

Yet, the Bible clearly teaches us that peace of mind is our heritage. It also teaches us how to obtain this peace of mind: "Do not fret or have any anxiety about anything, but in every circumstance and in everything, by prayer and petition (definite requests), with thanksgiving, continue to make your wants known to God. And God's peace [shall be yours, that tranquil state of a soul assured of its salvation through Christ, and so fearing nothing from God and being content with its earthly lot of whatever sort that is, that peace] which transcends all understanding shall garrison and mount guard over your hearts and minds in Christ Jesus" (Phil. 4:6–7).

Ask God to show you what is robbing you of peace, and then seek to reclaim your peace in that area.

So ask God to show you what is robbing you of peace, and then seek to reclaim your peace in that area. Keep in mind that if you want to live in peace, you must be willing to pay the price.

Be Willing to Pay the Price for Peace

Peace is glorious, but it would be unfair to you if I did not tell you that suffering is often the road to glory. Romans 8:17 brings this out clearly: "And if we are [His] children, then we are [His] heirs also: heirs of God and fellow heirs with Christ [sharing His inheritance with Him]; only we must share His suffering if we are to share His glory."

Jesus lives in glory at this very moment, but He had to suffer in order to get there. He had to die. He had to die to His own natural desires and live for His Father's will. Paul said, "I die daily" (1 Cor. 15:31). I believe he was saying, "There are a lot of things I would rather do, and things I would prefer not to do, but I say no and follow the spirit of God that is in me."

God has told us, "I set before you life and death; choose life" (Deut. 30:19, author's paraphrase). Making right choices can cause suffering when the flesh does not get its own way. The flesh ministers death, but the Spirit ministers life. If we follow our flesh, death is the result. If we follow the Spirit, the reward is life. Choosing peace instead of strife will certainly reward you with life and all the blessings that it brings. But, initially, you may have to say no to something your flesh wants.

For example, let's say I get up one morning and I am at peace. It is a lovely, sunny day, and I have nice plans that will bring enjoyment to me all day long. If everything goes the way I intend, all will be well. However, things begin to happen that threaten my plans to enjoy the day.

I receive a phone call from the office, informing me that our new phone system is not working properly and that a lot of our calls are not getting through. This information provides me with an opportunity. Will I worry—and choose death? Or will I pray and cast my care upon Jesus—and choose life?

If I cast my care on Jesus, I will stay at peace. If I give in to worry, I will start trying to figure out why this trouble happened and what I can do to make sure it does not happen again. I will think negative thoughts about the company we purchased the phone system from, and before long I will want to call and tell them what I think of them and their phone system. I will be agitated, fretful, touchy, and angry.

Remember, when I got up in the morning, everything was wonderful. If I let it, one phone call has the power to change my whole day and attitude. Making the right choice may cause me to suffer temporarily in some areas, but it will eventually produce peace and glory in many others.

Let peace have the deciding vote in the choices you make.

It's important to note that we often get out of balance in the area of suffering. Some Christians believe we glorify God by our suffering. They say, "Let's just love suffering and never resist any trouble." Others believe that Christians should never suffer, never be uncomfortable, and always get everything just the way they want it. However, we cannot live in the ditch on either side of the road of suffering. We need to steer our course straight down the middle of the road. We need balance—not extremes.

Suffering, in itself, does not glorify God. But if we are suffering in order to do His will, and if we maintain a proper attitude, our suffering will bring Him glory. Right choices will bring glory into our lives.

I now live in glorious peace most of the time. But I went through much suffering in order to come to this place. I had to learn to be quiet when I would rather keep talking. I had to learn to humble myself and apologize when I did not think I was wrong. As I made those right choices, my flesh suffered.

I had to be quiet when Dave thought he was right, when I would rather have argued and tried to prove that I had the answer. I had to walk away from conversations where people were being criticized and judged so that I could stay out of the strife I could sense. My flesh suffered because it was nosy and wanted to know everything. But the peace I now enjoy was worth the price.

So don't be afraid of "godly suffering." The apostle Paul wrote a letter to the Corinthians, saying something like this: "Even though my letter hurt you, I am not sorry that I wrote it because I know that later on it will produce good things in your life." (See 2 Corinthians 7:8.)

If you choose strife, you will suffer and end in defeat. Why not choose peace, which may provoke suffering in the flesh but will also lead to victory? If you are suffering because of strife, it will only lead to more suffering and greater problems. Why not choose to suffer in a godly way, knowing it will lead to glory?

Will You Make Peace the Umpire of Your Life?

No one could write a book big enough to cover every circumstance that you will face. But the Holy Spirit has come to administer the heritage that Jesus died to give you. God wants you to live in peace; He wants to unleash His power and His blessings in your life. But the final choice is yours.

Will you make peace the umpire of your life?

An umpire makes the decision that settles the matter. Each team may believe the call should be in its own favor, but it is the umpire who makes the final decision. And once he does, that ends the matter.

Let peace have the deciding vote in the choices you make. If something does not bring you peace, cast it out. Don't live for the moment only. Use wisdom to make choices now that will satisfy you later on. When you are having a difficult time hearing from God or being able to decide what you should do in a certain situation, follow after peace.

Colossians 3:15 tells us, "And let the peace (soul harmony which comes) from Christ rule (act as umpire continually) in your hearts [deciding and settling with finality all questions that arise in your minds, in that peaceful state] to which as [members of Christ's] one body you were also called [to live]. And be thankful (appreciative), [giving praise to God always]."

You have a unique call upon your life. You are an important part of the body of Christ. God has prearranged for you to have a powerful and productive life. Jesus paid for it. It is yours unless you allow the devil to steal it from you.

Make a decision today: "I am finished with upset and turmoil; peace is mine, and I am going to enjoy it now," and begin to live in peace. Keep conflict out of your life; out of your thoughts, words, and attitudes; out of your relationships. Choose life! Choose peace!

Chapter 15
Summary and Reflection

We are heirs of Christ, according to God's Word. Jesus said, "Everything that the Father has is Mine. That is what I meant when I said that He [the Spirit] will take the things that are Mine and will reveal (declare, disclose, transmit) it to you" (John 16:15).

Even though we have a rich, wonderful, and powerful inheritance in Christ, far too few of us ever walk in what He has given to us. To reclaim our inheritance, we need to maintain trouble-free relationships.

1. According to John 14:27, peace was a part of Jesus Christ's last will and testament to His people. If Jesus Christ spoke of peace right before He died, how important do you think peace is in His estimation?

_____

_____

2. Read Philippians 4:6–7 and describe one biblical way for holding on to your peace.

_____

_____

3. Are you living in peace with yourself, others, and God? If so, explain why you have been able to do so. If not, ask God to reveal what is robbing you of peace and what you need to do to be a peacemaker.

_____

_____

4. List some ways you have chosen to deny your fleshly desires and keep peace in a relationship.

_____

_____

5. Think about your day today. Describe how you either chose peace, and avoided strife and conflict, or those times when you gave in to strife. What was the result?

_____

_____

6. Will you make the decision today to make peace the umpire of your life? Write out a prayer, telling God of your commitment to do so.

_____

_____

_____

_____

_____

_____

Dear Lord, help me to make peace the umpire of my life in all of my relationships. Show me more and more biblical strategies for maintaining peace. Holy Spirit, nudge me when strife attempts to enter into my heart and mind. Show me how to diffuse every situation with faith, love, confidence, and joy. In Jesus's name, amen.

Bibliography

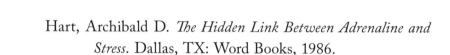

Hart, Archibald D. *The Hidden Link Between Adrenaline and Stress*. Dallas, TX: Word Books, 1986.

Strong, James. *The New Strong's Exhaustive Concordance of the Bible*. Nashville, TN: Thomas Nelson Publishers, 1990.

Vine, W. E., *Vine's Complete Expository Dictionary of Old and New Testament Words*. Nashville, TN: Thomas Nelson Publishers, 1985.

Webster's II New Riverside University Dictionary. Boston, MA: Houghton Mifflin Company, 1994.

About the Author

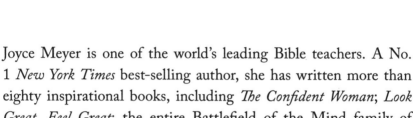

Joyce Meyer is one of the world's leading Bible teachers. A No. 1 *New York Times* best-selling author, she has written more than eighty inspirational books, including *The Confident Woman*; *Look Great, Feel Great*; the entire Battlefield of the Mind family of books; and many others. She has also released thousands of audio teachings as well as a complete video library. Joyce's *Enjoying Everyday Life* radio and television programs are broadcast around the world, and she travels extensively conducting conferences. Joyce and her husband, Dave, are the parents of four grown children and make their home in St. Louis, Missouri.

Other Books by Joyce Meyer

The Penny

The Power of Simple Prayer

The Everyday Life Bible (hardcover or bonded leather)

The Confident Woman

Look Great, Feel Great

Battlefield of the Mind *

Battlefield of the Mind Devotional

Battlefield of the Mind for Teens

Battlefield of the Mind for Kids

Approval Addiction

Ending Your Day Right

21 Ways to Finding Peace and Happiness

The Secret Power of Speaking God's Word

Seven Things That Steal Your Joy

Starting Your Day Right

Beauty for Ashes (revised edition)

How to Hear from God *

Knowing God Intimately

The Power of Forgiveness

The Power of Determination

The Power of Being Positive

The Secrets of Spiritual Power

The Battle Belongs to the Lord

The Secrets to Exceptional Living

Eight Ways to Keep the Devil Under Your Feet

Teenagers Are People Too!

Filled With the Spirit

Celebration of Simplicity

The Joy of Believing Prayer

Never Lose Heart

Being the Person God Made You to Be

A Leader in the Making

"Good Morning, This Is God!" (gift book)

Jesus—Name Above All Names

Making Marriage Work
(Previously published as *Help Me—I'm Married!*)

Reduce Me to Love

Be Healed in Jesus' Name

How to Succeed at Being Yourself

Weary Warriors, Fainting Saints

Be Anxious for Nothing *

Straight Talk Omnibus

Don't Dread

Managing Your Emotions

Healing the Brokenhearted

Me and My Big Mouth! *

Prepare to Prosper

Do It Afraid!

Expect a Move of God in Your Life . . . Suddenly!

Enjoying Where You Are on the Way to Where You Are Going

A New Way of Living

When, God, When?

Why, God, Why?

The Word, the Name, the Blood

Tell Them I Love Them

Peace

If Not for the Grace of God *

Joyce Meyer Spanish Titles

Las Siete Cosas Que Te Roban el Gozo
(Seven Things That Steal Your Joy)

Empezando Tu Dia Bien
(Starting Your Day Right)

* Study Guide available for this title.

Books by Dave Meyer

Life Lines